"Judy Salisbury's book is a powerful tool for the defense of the faith, one that combines fascinating facts with true spiritual understanding and a refreshing sense of humor. Judy encourages, exhorts, and powerfully persuades us to remember how vitally important it is to understand why we believe."

Jill Martin Rische,
cofounder of Walter Martin's Religious InfoNet
and coauthor of *Through the Windows of Heaven*

"Judy Salisbury is a gifted writer and teacher whose work and life exhibit the ideal combination of intellectual integrity with an attractive, gracious, and winsome personality. Her latest work is an important contribution to the cause of Christ in our world. I highly recommend it."

Francis J. Beckwith,
author of *Relativism: Feet Firmly Planted in Mid-Air*
and Associate Professor of Church-State Studies, Baylor University

"There are many books available that teach mothers how to raise their children in a godly way, but this is the first I've seen that equips them to answer their children's spiritual questions with biblical insight and accuracy. The author's practical, day-to-day illustrations give the reader a deeper understanding of Scripture and a desire to ask the hard questions that will bring God and His Word more into focus. This book will prepare every woman, wife, or mother to answer those one-on-one questions brought to them by their children, friends, family members, or even complete strangers."

Sally E. Stuart,
author of *Christian Writer's Market Guide*

"Judy Salisbury's unique approach to Christian apologetics gives the reader a firm foundation—and in a society of relativism, it's nice to know there is an Absolute we can cling to. Judy not only reminds us to remember our first love, the Lord Jesus Christ, but also illustrates that love by way of her often humorous and always thought-provoking examples. A must-read for believers and seekers alike."

Joan Phillips,
author of *Her Choice to Heal*

A CHRISTIAN WOMAN'S GUIDE TO

Reasons for Faith

JUDY SALISBURY

HARVEST HOUSE™ PUBLISHERS

EUGENE, OREGON

Cover by Terry Dugan Design, Minneapolis, Minnesota

A CHRISTIAN WOMAN'S GUIDE TO REASONS FOR FAITH

Copyright © 2003 by Judy Salisbury
Published by Harvest House Publishers
Eugene, Oregon 97402

Library of Congress Cataloging-in-Publication Data

Salisbury, Judy, 1963-
  A Christian Woman's guide to reasons for faith / Judy Salisbury.
      p. cm.
Includes bibliographical references.
  ISBN 0-7369-1127-8 (pbk.)
  1. Christian women—Religious life. I. Title.
BV4527.S235 2003
239' . 082—dc21

                                                          2003001886

Printed in the United States of America

        03 04 05 06 07 08 09 10 11 / BP-MS / 10 9 8 7 6 5 4 3 2 1

To my darling daughter,

*N*icole:

*Retain the standard of sound words which you have heard from me,
in the faith and love which are in Christ Jesus.
Guard, through the Holy Spirit who dwells in us,
the treasure which has been entrusted to you.*

—2 Timothy 1:13-14

Acknowledgments

My deepest appreciation and very special thanks to Dr. Norman Geisler for encouraging me to write this book, and for his most gracious foreword. My humble thanks to the apologists who've dedicated their lives to providing wonderful resources that help us everyday, nonscholarly folk offer sound reasons for our faith; their names and resources you will find throughout this book.

Many thanks to Darlene Ankerberg and Dr. Ron Carlson for referring me to Harvest House Publishers.

My very special thanks to Harvest House Publishers for moving forward with this unique project. What a pleasure it is to be a part of the family! Special thanks to Terry Glaspey and Carolyn McCready for their insight from the start, and to Barbara Sherrill for her invaluable suggestions. My humble thanks to my editor, Paul Gossard, one of the most gracious individuals I have ever worked with. I thank God for his intellect, instinct, and instruction.

Thanks also to Professor Frank Sherwin for his input on chapter 5 and for his timely answers to a myriad of questions, and to Dr. Duane Gish for taking the time to review chapter 5 as well.

Special thanks to the Hubbell family for sharing their immense love and powerful testimony. To my dear friends Connie and Nan, who ask me the deepest and most challenging questions, thank you for keeping me on my spiritual and intellectual toes! I am truly indebted to many brothers and sisters in Christ at Calvary Chapel, Vancouver, Washington, and Pleasant View Community Church, Ariel, Washington, for their prayers, love, and support of my ministry. Thank you so, so much; your humility and service to the Lord are jewels in your ever-growing crowns.

Special thanks also to my understanding and patient children, Nicole and Mikael, the best reasons to become equipped with reasons. To my beloved Jeff, thank you for your unwavering passionate and compassionate love for me; how wonderful that we are still best friends.

To my Lord and Savior Jesus Christ—how thankful I am that the foolishness of God is wiser than men; for if it wasn't, I'd never stand a chance (Acts 4:13). May You alone be glorified.

Contents

Foreword

by Dr. Norm Geisler

Do you have reasons for your faith? As Christians, it is vitally important that we do. Yet, for many years, I have had a growing concern over the lack of available and appropriate resources specifically designed for women, written by women, in the area of Christian apologetics.

Simply put, Christian apologetics is the ministry of offering sound reasons for the Faith to those who have a variety of questions, believer and unbeliever alike. Since women, and especially mothers, seem to have the greatest number of spontaneous opportunities to share and defend their faith, filling this need is crucial.

What a breath of fresh air it was to meet a woman who knows how to do what the Bible commands each of us to do, yet in a way that "puts the cookies on the bottom shelf." Judy Salisbury is a trained professional speaker and a competent defender of the Christian Faith, as well as a dedicated wife and mother. Her message not only transforms the heart, but it satisfies the mind.

I know of no book on the market that better meets the spiritual needs and fills the intellectual hunger of women who want to see their friends, family, and children in the kingdom of God than *A Christian Woman's Guide to Reasons for Faith*. Judy not only writes in an engaging, dynamic, and biblical way, but her commonsense answers also will help mothers—and fathers too—prepare their children for the pagan and anti-Christian world in which they find themselves. After all, studies show that children who grow up without good reasons for the faith of the parents tend to discard it in high percentages while in college.

In short, this book is a stimulating, informative, oftentimes witty, and encouraging resource for women with a desire to impact their sphere of influence for the Lord Jesus Christ in a manner that indeed reaches the heart, soul, and mind.

Dr. Norman L. Geisler, President
Southern Evangelical Seminary
Charlotte, North Carolina

Opportunities Are Everywhere

☙

God has a sense of humor. I never really knew, until recently, how careful a woman should be about whining too loudly or too often—because she just might be the one God taps on the shoulder to meet the challenge.

For a long time I grumbled in front of the apologetics section (or the woman's section) in Christian bookstores, unable to get ahold of a resource that would help equip me with reasons for my faith while addressing my spiritual and emotional needs as well. I thought, *Wouldn't it be great to find a resource without sports analogies that I can't understand because I don't play golf or football, but rather includes stories I can relate to—stories that will help me remember a particular answer or spiritual truth?* Well, I guess this book is an example of "she who complains the most will find herself engaged in the task."

Several things have motivated me to become better equipped with reasons for my faith. One of them was that it simply amazed me, shortly after I had given my life to the Lord Jesus Christ, how everyone suddenly seemed to be talking about spiritual matters. (Perhaps it's like when you buy a car—somehow, everyone seems to be driving the same model.) Because spiritual matters seemed to be the talk of the town, I felt I needed a resource to help me become better equipped.

You may well feel the same. Opportunities abound with friends, family, neighbors, grocery-store clerks, co-workers, doctors...and the list can go on and on. For example, I never in my life had a cultist knock on my door until I gave my life to Christ. After that, I thought my doorbell had a magnet on it! (This is not why we later moved to the woods.)

Opportunities All Around

Even before giving my life to Christ, I had vast numbers of opportunities to discuss spiritual matters with hurting or searching individuals all around me. I wish I could relive those spontaneous divine appointments that just seemed to fall into my lap back then. I would enthusiastically seize them today. Unfortunately, though I considered myself a Christian, my heart was far from Christ. In the yesterdays of my pursuit of self rather than a relationship with God or others, my career in corporate sales took center stage in my life, along with aspirations to become an entertainer (comedy, to be exact).

My Missed Divine Opportunities

There was one individual in particular, a sales assistant who I will call Lance, who was about as open as anyone could be to discussing spiritual matters. There were about eight of us sales folk who he would assist with basic secretarial duties. I had a soft spot in my heart for Lance, yet I was insensitive to his spiritual hunger.

I will never forget how, every Monday morning for the first three months I worked for that particular corporation, I would blow through the office doors, scuttle past Lance's desk with a hot cup of tea, and go straight to my desk so I could hit the phones to set appointments for the week. The next time anyone would see a glimpse of me would be on Fridays, when I would yet again blow past everyone with a straight-faced, monotone "morning," and disappear into my cubicle until late in the evening to complete paperwork and follow-up on customers or prospects.

My whole demeanor was strictly business, and everyone around me knew it. Within my first year I had won two national sales awards and landed the company's first three international contracts. Because

I appeared so focused, this prompted my co-workers to keep their distance. However, one day, all that changed.

"Good morning, everyone!" I practically sang as I whirled by Lance with a single red rose in my hand, one that I had discovered on my car that morning. "It's a great day, isn't it?" My assistant's jaw almost hit his desk. No, I hadn't met the Lord Jesus Christ just yet...I had just met my husband, Jeff. I will never forget how people wandered out of their cubicles and offices with the same disoriented look on their faces as Lance while I, without being asked, jubilantly told everyone in earshot about the wonderful time I had had with this *guy* who had taken me to the de Young Museum in San Francisco. A light had entered my life, and it brought me to share a tiny bit of myself with others. (It's funny how a thing like being madly in love can change you. How much more so when falling in love with the Light of the world—it sure is hard to keep silent about our relationship with Him, isn't it?)

Well, the change had a positive effect on everyone, it seemed. Soon I was having lunch with the gang at work, and I even elected to change my schedule to attend company-paid ball games and a variety of outings. After a while, the other sales staff didn't mind joking with me about how standoffish I had been before I had met the man I would marry just seven short months later.

Lance seemed to be the happiest for me when he heard that Jeff and I had impulsively eloped. He said assuredly, "You two must have known each other in a past life—that's why you connected so quickly." To which I quipped, "Lance, this world could only handle me once. I guarantee you I never had a past life." Oh, how I wish we could have that conversation now.

I also remember hearing one of the other sales reps repeatedly in tears on the telephone with her ex-husband, begging him for cooperation and help with their four children. Daily I could see she carried a heavy weight, yet she turned to the stars for answers. I don't think she ever got them. Since I wasn't equipped at the time, she certainly didn't get any from me.

Perhaps you've had the same experience. A friend or co-worker, desperately needing the Savior's touch, tugs at your heart but you hesitate because you feel ill-equipped to answer her concerns. You may wonder, *Where and how do I even begin the task?* My dear sister, God has not only provided you with a wonderful opportunity to share, but now you have a resource that can help you do that confidently and competently.

My 360° Life and Attitude Change

How sad for me that, unlike many Christian women, I did not recognize the need to reach those around me with the truth they obviously longed for. Through life's circumstances, God had to bring me to my knees in a little hotel room by way of a Gideon Bible. There I truly gave Him my life. Yet again, I was in for a huge life and attitude change. Truly a transformation of heart, mind, soul, and yes—career. As you can probably imagine, this particular life change quickly brought about new opportunities to share my faith.

Three-and-a-half years after Jeff and I had eloped, the physical birth of our daughter, Nicole, came on Christmas Eve—almost exactly one year after my spiritual birth. She was huge—10 lbs., 3 oz.—but she was still our tiny little baby girl. Once the swelling in her face had subsided, my husband was right—she was exquisite. Since I had never had the opportunity to baby-sit, I was somewhat embarrassed to ask the nurses—at almost 30 years of age—"Now, just *how* do I change that diaper?" I learned quickly.

I'll never forget snuggling with her on the couch, reflecting on what seemed like a full year that I had carried her. Now, here she was in my arms. After a few days, Jeff felt safe enough to return to work and leave me alone with Nicole, fully confident that I had mastered diaper-changing. I had no ambivalence or misgivings for having left the corporate world for the precious little bundle I snuggled close to me. For I recognized that God had entrusted to me my highest and richest calling. He had made me Nicole's mommy.

So many thoughts flooded my mind. But as I looked at her tiny face and delicate little hands, I must say the most compelling thought was the realization that she was going to ask serious questions about our faith and beliefs. It did not take a pediatrician or a parenting class to tell me that one day she was going to ask "Why?" *How awful it would be,* I thought, *for her to turn to someone else besides her mommy and daddy for the answers.* At this point in my relationship with the

Lord, I was acutely aware that there were others who would just love to give her answers that would sound good on the surface, but would lead her to spiritual death. When I thought back on my days in corporate sales, I could not imagine the pain of seeing my daughter swept away, as the daughters of several of my colleagues were.

I was so thankful I had spent the first year of my Christian infancy reading the Holy Bible cover to cover. What a wonderful experience it was! Prophecies regarding the long-awaited Messiah seemed to jump off the pages. I had never realized just how many common expressions, such as "the handwriting is on the wall," had actually come from the Bible. They were certainly fun to discover. More importantly, I learned parenting skills, which I desperately needed, from the perfect heavenly Parent. And I began to know and draw closer to the God in whom I had finally put my trust.

Now, I know this won't come as a surprise to you, but by age three Nicole was off and running with "Why this…?" "Why that…?" "How come…?" As a new believer, I too had a million questions, and I began the arduous task of becoming equipped. For me it was arduous because, by the end of the day with a little one, I found that my mind was downright fried. Yet God was faithful to answer my prayers when I cried to Him for help in understanding the material I felt compelled to study.

A Place to Start

What you have in your hand is a bit of fruit from my study effort. This book was born out of a desire to better understand what I believe. It was born out of a desire to help others meet our risen Lord. It was born out of a deep desire to offer my children sound reasons for our faith. Finally, it was born out of a desire to help Christian women who wish to become equipped, but who simply need a safe, practical, relatable, and fun place to start.

I sincerely think you will find this book an asset when sharing your love for Jesus Christ, His Word, His truth, and His offer of eternal life with others. It is a resource that will help you answer your children's concerns as well as the concerns of the friends they bring across the threshold of your home. It is a resource that will help you reach your friends and co-workers who are seeking something…Someone.

It is a wonderful blessing to offer sound answers to those who want and need them. But my further hope and prayer is that you will find that understanding *why* you believe *what* you believe will actually strengthen and ground you to face even life's most turbulent storms. So, pop some popcorn, make a nice hot cup of cocoa, slip a peppermint stick into it...and may the Lord richly bless you as you become better equipped with basic, sound, simple, memorable reasons for your faith.

Your sister and servant in Christ,
Judy Salisbury
February 2003

PART ONE

The Most Common
Questions

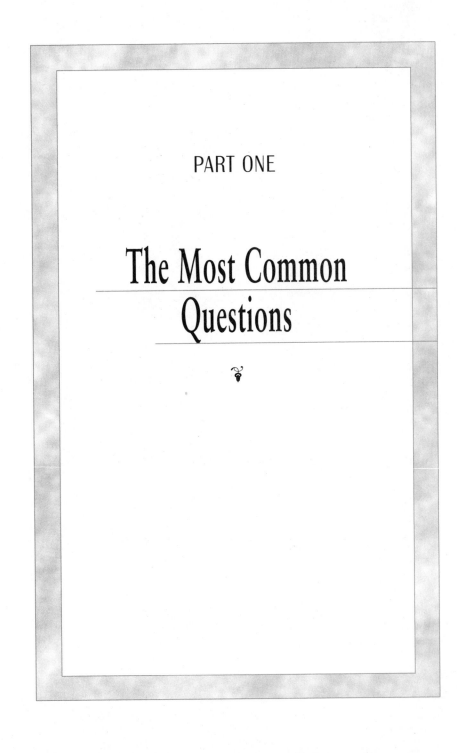

CHAPTER 1

Trusting the Word

"God said it. I believe it. That settles it." A rather bold saying, to be sure. However, when I was a new believer, though I was without a doubt committed to the Lord Jesus Christ, I was somewhat apprehensive about committing to trust the Bible as well. I realized that if I was to grow closer to God and know His will for my life, the Bible was the place to turn. But just like so many others, I had questions...and yes, concerns. One of which was if the Bible was truly God's Word.

Thankfully, our merciful and loving heavenly Parent did not leave us without answers. He did not give us a burning desire to seek for Him and grope for Him (according to Acts 17:27), only to leave us frustrated in our quest to find Him. God, in His immense love for His image-bearers, gave not just what so many refer to as *Life's Little Instruction Book*—no, it is so much more than that. God has given us His very Word, a window to His heart and to His love for fallen humanity, which we call the Holy Bible.

Is it okay to question the validity of the Bible? Is it okay to have doubts? Is it okay to wonder if it is really any different from other holy books from the vast array of world religions? In a nutshell, is it okay to ask, "Why?" or, "Why should we believe that the Holy Bible is the inspired Word of God?"

Of course it's okay to ask these questions, because God loves to prove Himself true. Since, thankfully, the answers are so plentiful, I will share just a few points from several areas. First, I'd like to look at some basic misconceptions regarding the Bible. Second, I'll discuss the reliability of the Old and New Testament manuscripts. Third, I'll share some fascinating biblical prophecies and their fulfillment. Fourth, we'll look at Jesus' attitude toward the Scriptures and how He used them. Lastly, I'll share just a few thoughts on the importance of the Word of God in our lives.

The Bible: Must Reading

Truly, one can turn to the Holy Bible for life's little instructions. And if we turned to it for this purpose alone, to help us on our day-to-day journey through life, it would certainly be a worthy read. Unfortunately, though it is the most widely purchased book in North America, it is still the least read. One of the things that amazed me as a new believer—and still does—is just how many professing Christians have never read their Bible cover to cover. However, I am just as amazed at the number of individuals who disbelieve it who, likewise, have never read it. It is no wonder that so many people have a difficult time defending or refuting it when this is the case.

Therefore, due to the dust buildup on many a Bible, I think there are several misconceptions I should briefly touch upon to perhaps help strengthen our confidence when presenting the Bible to others.

Common Misconceptions About Divine Inspiration

I think it could be possible that those who feel a bit ambivalent about the Bible's trustworthiness just might picture a bunch of guys in tunics sitting around jawing about a great book idea that could change the world. That somehow a bunch of guys with overactive imaginations made the whole thing up. Perhaps the ambivalent folks might even think that some wise guys offered their own interpretation of what God communicated. However, the apostle Peter assures us that this is not the case. In classic passionate Peter fashion he emphatically states, "But know this first of all, that no prophecy of Scripture is a matter of one's own interpretation, for no prophecy was ever made by an act of human will, but men moved by the Holy Spirit spoke from God."[1]

Then we get a bit more help from the apostle Paul, who explains how the Spirit of God communicated to him and the other apostles, and why believers who hear the message can recognize it as being from the Spirit of God.

> *We have received, not the spirit of the world, but the Spirit who is from God, so that we may know the things freely given to us by God, which things we also speak, not in words taught by human wisdom, but in those taught by the Spirit, combining spiritual thoughts with spiritual words [or, "interpreting spiritual things to spiritual men"]. But a natural man [or, "an unspiritual" man] does not accept the things of the Spirit of God, for they are foolishness to him; and he cannot understand them, because they are spiritually appraised.[2]*

Second Timothy 3:16 states that "all Scripture is inspired by God." Now, while that seems pretty straightforward, what does it really mean? The word *inspired* in the Greek literally means *God-breathed*. The word *all* means just that—*all!* Not some, not pick-and-choose, but *"all* Scripture is inspired by God."

To sum up the above passages, all Scripture was given by the Holy Spirit of God, who inspired individuals of His choosing, at a time of His choosing, to write. And, as believers, we can grasp the Scriptures by the Holy Spirit as well. Therefore, while many individuals write beautifully inspiring messages or songs, it is quite another matter to claim that what was written was divinely inspired.

For example, if you were holding two "holy books," one in either hand, there would be ways of knowing which one of them was truly inspired by God, if either. Since no two contradictory statements can both be true at the same time and in the same sense, the first question to ask is, "Do the messages contained in these books contradict each other?" If one states, for example, that you are to worship many gods, yet the Bible states that there is only one true and living God who said, "You shall have no other gods before Me," then obviously there is a contradiction. Both books cannot be true on the subject of God and worship. Hence, it would be time to put these books to the test. That is exactly the purpose of this chapter: to discover if the "Good Book" really was written through divine inspiration.

Tough Stuff: More Common Misconceptions

I find that, while we are more than happy to get the Word of God into the hands of eager seekers, there are some topics in the Bible that just might make us bristle when we're confronted with them. The following are just a few of the prickly items that often rock the believer and rouse the unbeliever.

1. Slavery

The subject of slavery is always a sticky one, yet it is often misunderstood when we consider biblical times. Though it was part of the culture at that time, thankfully it was far from what we imagine when we think of slavery today. Some individuals actually became slaves as a means of paying their debts—however, the Bible does not advocate abuse but states that slaves were to be treated with dignity and respect. For example, if a slave ran away from his master, he was able to live where he wished without fear of being returned.[3] Job, for example, recognized that he and his slaves were equal before God, and he understood that if he mistreated them he would stand accountable before God for that mistreatment. In his words:

> *If I have despised the claim of my male or female slaves*
> *When they filed a complaint against me,*
> *What then could I do when God arises?*
> *And when He calls me to account, what will I answer Him?*
> *Did not He who made me in the womb make him,*
> *And the same one fashion us in the womb?*[4]

2. Bigamy

The practice of bigamy as recorded in the Bible, is another issue that certainly, and rightfully, causes concern. We might well ask, if Solomon's wealth and wisdom were a gift from God, how could he have chosen to have so many wives? Yet Solomon's wayward lusts led to his despair and demise. The book of Ecclesiastes, which he penned, expresses his view of the self-indulgent life quite appropriately. "Vanity of vanities! All is vanity."[5] Quite literally, "Futility of futilities! All is futile." Solomon's lust for women drew his heart away from God.

When God spoke on the subject of matrimony, an institution created by Him, He was very clear regarding His intent: "A man shall leave his father and his mother, and be joined to his wife [singular]; and they shall become *one flesh*."[6]

As I look at the lives of Bible characters, it seems to me that the departure from God's standard for marriage by those who pursued the cultural practice of bigamy brought nothing but trouble. Who can forget the rivalry of Rachel and Leah—yet they were the mothers of the children of Israel. God redeemed the human circumstance that resulted from sin by bringing about a great nation. Though we never read that God condoned the practice, it seems that He may have simply tolerated bigamy as a part of Israel's culture for only a season.

3. Other Sordid Events

We would have to agree that, aside from bigamy or slavery, there are several unflattering and at times ungodly circumstances that are recorded in the Bible. Abraham embroidering the truth before King Abimelech in regard to Sarah being his sister rather than his bride, or Leah purchasing from Rachel a night with Jacob for a handful of mandrakes. And of course, who can ever forget the David–Bathsheba affair?

Actually, when you think about it, the fact that Bible characters are not pictured in their best light—but in their frailty, during their not-so-godly decisions—certainly affords more credence to the Scriptures. The events are simply reported as they actually happened. You can be sure that if the Scriptures had been contrived, many a biblical character would be portrayed as the supersaint of the century. However many, like all of us, were far from that. Peter, for example, constantly put his foot in his mouth, and in a very cowardly way he swore that he did not know Jesus—not once but three times. What a failure on the part of the man who had promised our Lord just hours before that if everyone else deserted Him, he alone would die for Him! Yet we all have our Peter moments, don't we? Thanks be to God for His immediate forgiveness and restoration when we seek it.

4. Seeming Inconsistencies

Sometimes, spotting an inconsistency in the Scriptures can sure knock us for a loop. For example, in the Gospel of Mark it is stated that Jesus was crucified at the third hour. But John's account states that at the sixth hour Jesus was still on trial! Both can't be true—or can they? This little difficulty is easily explained by Dr. Norman Geisler and Thomas Howe in their most handy resource *When Critics Ask: A Popular Handbook on Bible Difficulties:*

> Both Gospel writers are correct in their assertions. The difficulty is answered when we realize that each Gospel writer used a different time system. John follows the *Roman* time system while Mark follows the *Jewish* time system.
>
> According to Roman time, the day ran from midnight to midnight. The Jewish 24-hour period began in the evening at 6 P.M. and the morning of that day began at 6 A.M. Therefore, when Mark asserts that at the third hour Christ was crucified, this was about 9 A.M. John stated that Christ's trial was about the sixth hour [6 A.M. Roman time]. This would place the trial *before* the crucifixion and this would not negate any testimony of the Gospel writers.[7]

Indeed, it seems to make more sense for John to use Roman time, since he was writing a Gospel to the Gentiles. Mark, documenting the words of Peter, was writing from a more Jewish perspective (considering the fact that Mark's Gospel opens with a quotation from Isaiah).

In any case, while there are some variations in the records of the same event, the variations are not contradictions. Moreover, there are always variations in eyewitness testimony. The variations don't discredit the validity of the accounts—in actuality, the variations in the biblical accounts *validate* the Scriptures. I imagine that if all the accounts were identically written, word for word, we might well suspect the authors of collaboration.

In sum, any apparent inconsistencies in the Bible are just that— *apparent*. What we might perceive as an inconsistency or contradiction can be understood by taking into account the language, idioms, customs, or culture of that time.

Are the Old Testament Texts Reliable?

Remember the telephone game? Someone whispers something in your ear, and you whisper it in the next person's ear, and so on until the message travels all around the room. By the time the message reaches the last person it is dramatically different from the original. When I played the game, I just couldn't resist the temptation to alter the original message to something rather silly and bizarre. Why? Because it's a game—and the more the message changes the funnier the game becomes.

Unfortunately, some people are of the opinion that relying on the Scriptures is like relying on the last person in the telephone game. They believe that each time the text was copied it may have been altered from the original message. However, since Old Testament scribes understood their task as copying what God had breathed, they viewed it as anything but a game, as Dr. Geisler aptly notes:

> With respect to the Jewish Scriptures, however, it was not scribal accuracy alone that guaranteed their product. Rather, it was their almost superstitious reverence for the Bible. According to the *Talmud* there were specifications not only for the kind of skins to be used and the size of the columns, but there was even a religious ritual necessary for the scribe to perform before writing the name of God. Rules governed the kind of ink used, dictated the spacing of words, and prohibited writing anything from memory. The lines, and even the letters, were counted methodically. If a manuscript was found to contain even one mistake, it was discarded and destroyed. This scribal formalism was responsible, at least in part, for the extreme care exercised in copying the Scriptures. It was also the reason there were only a few manuscripts (as the rules demanded the destruction of defective copies).[8]

Perhaps you've heard of the Dead Sea Scrolls and wondered what was so significant about the find. Well, among the scrolls discovered in 1947 at Qumran was the entire book of Isaiah. This scroll turned out to be about a thousand years older than the oldest manuscript of Isaiah available at the time. Proving Dr. Geisler's point, it is word-for-word identical to our standard Hebrew text today. Due to the meticulousness of the scribes, overall our Old Testament Scriptures are 95-percent pure. The 5-percent variation is only in punctuation or spelling, nothing that would affect any major doctrine.

What About the New Testament Manuscripts?

When we consider the reliability of the New Testament, it is important to note that it was written entirely during the first century A.D. Why is this important? Since the majority of the New Testament was written between A.D. 47 and 70, those who might be concerned about legends creeping into the text can put their mind at ease. The time span between the documentation of the events and the actual events was simply too short for legend to have developed. Since many of Jesus' contemporaries were still alive at the time of the writing of the text, these individuals would have recognized anything false as legend and would have been able to refute it immediately.

Though there are various ways of proving that the New Testament was written between A.D. 47 and 70, I'll share just one way for simplicity's sake. We can know approximately when the New Testament Scriptures were written by what is *not* recorded. For example, you would think that the destruction of Jerusalem and the temple and the dispersion of the Jewish people by the Roman general Titus in A.D. 70 might get even a little mention had the events occurred before the texts were written. It would be like me writing a book on the recent history of America and omitting September 11, 2001. Since the events of that day so dramatically impacted our whole country, surely you would have to assume that my omission was because of the fact that my writing came before the horrific events of that memorable day.

The other exciting little item to note is that there is a time lapse of only 100 to 200 years between the original writing of the New Testament and the oldest copies we have of it. In contrast, the time frame between Plato's original writings and the oldest existing copies is approximately 1200 years. In the case of Aristotle there are approximately 1400 years between his original writings and the most ancient copies, and for Homer's *Iliad* we have about a 500-year gap.[9] Therefore, if we can accept the texts of Plato, Aristotle, and Homer as authentic, surely we can trust the New Testament texts as well—especially since the New Testament is 99.5-percent pure in its accuracy to the original. As with the Old Testament, there are variations in style or spelling, but nothing that would affect any major doctrine.

Of all the works of antiquity, the New Testament has the greatest amount of surviving manuscript evidence. With a whopping 24,000 ancient manuscript copies of the New Testament, comparisons bear out the accuracy of the text. No other ancient writing even comes close. For Plato's writings, there are less than 10 ancient manuscript copies, for Aristotle, 50, and for Homer's *Iliad*, approximately 640 surviving manuscript copies.

Rest assured that the Gospels of Matthew, Mark, and John are documented eyewitness accounts. And though Luke, the author of the Gospel of Luke and the Acts of the Apostles, was not an eyewitness, the good doctor was a meticulous historian. It is widely acknowledged that Luke's background information is historically, geographically, and archeologically verifiable.

How Would the Psychic Hot Line Fare Against Biblical Prophecy?

Since questions regarding the future occupy the minds of many people, biblical prophecy is by far one of the most exciting proofs for the reliability of the Holy Bible. Prophecy truly sets the Bible apart from any other holy book of the world religions—and it sets the Bible's God apart from any other so-called god, as Isaiah 46:9-11 reveals:

> *Remember the former things long past,*
> *For I am God, and there is no other;*
> *I am God, and there is no one like Me,*
> *Declaring the end from the beginning,*
> *And from ancient times things which have not been done,*
> *Saying, "My purpose will be established,*
> *And I will accomplish all my good pleasure";*
> *Calling a bird of prey from the east,*
> *The man of My purpose from a far country.*
> *Truly I have spoken; truly I will bring it to pass.*
> *I have planned it, surely I will do it.*

He has indeed declared "the end from the beginning, and from ancient times things which have not been done" because, as Psalm 103:19 proclaims,

> *The LORD has established His throne in the heavens,*
> *And His sovereignty rules over all.*

Incredibly detailed biblical prophecies concerning cities like Sidon, Samaria, Gaza, Edom—and the list can go on—have been fulfilled in explicit detail. So precise and accurate are the prophecies recorded in the book of Daniel—including the succession of the empires of Babylon, Medo–Persia, Greece, and Rome—that some critics have made the unsubstantiated claim that the book was written after the events took place. Unfortunately for these critics, the dating of the book of Daniel is historically verifiable.

A Prophecy About a City

I think you just might agree that one of the most fascinating predictions concerned a city called Tyre. In Ezekiel 26, several interesting prophecies were decreed by God against this city, which included the following:

- King Nebuchadnezzar of Babylon would besiege the mainland city of Tyre.

- The city walls would be destroyed, the towers broken down, and the debris of the city would be scraped down to the bare rock.

- The stones, timber, and debris from the city would be thrown into the water.

- It would become a place for fishermen to spread their nets.

- The city would never again be rebuilt.

In 585 B.C., three years after Ezekiel's dramatic prophecy, King Nebuchadnezzar began a 13-year siege of mainland Tyre. By 573 B.C., mainland Tyre was completely destroyed. Several hundred years later, the Tyrians who lived on the island city bruised the ego of Alexander the Great by refusing to open their gates upon his request to do so. Irate at their refusal, Alex proceeded to besiege the city. Since he did not possess a naval fleet at the time, he had the debris of mainland Tyre literally scraped into the sea, thus building a causeway to the island city of Tyre and leaving mainland Tyre a bare rock. The mainland city has never been rebuilt, and if you decide to go there for your next vacation, you will find fishermen drying their nets upon the shore.

As I looked into this intriguing prophecy, I became a bit more curious and wanted to find out what Tyre looked like today. So I perused the Internet and came across a visitor's guide. The Web site mentioned something I found most interesting. "Whether it was the Hellenistic, Roman, or Byzantine conquerors of the ancient world or the Crusaders and Ottomans of the Middle Ages, they all came and went, like the ebb and flow of Tyre's beautiful shoreline." Now, you might be thinking, *What's so interesting about that?* Well, it just happens to be yet another prophecy fulfilled. Ezekiel 26:3 reads, "Thus says the Lord GOD, 'Behold, I am against you, O Tyre, and I will bring up many nations against you, as the sea brings up its waves.'"

Specific Prophecies About Specific People

There are scores of biblical prophecies concerning events, such as the return of the Jewish people to their homeland from around the globe, the deserts of Israel agriculturally flourishing, and the increase of communication, knowledge, and travel in the last days.

There is also a variety of prophecies about individuals—including, of course, the long-awaited Messiah (I will go over some of these in a later chapter). For now, let's take a look at what the Lord declared in Isaiah 44:28 concerning one man in particular, a man named Cyrus.

> *It is I who says of Cyrus, "He is my shepherd!*
> *And he will perform all My desire."*
> *And he declares of Jerusalem, "She will be built,"*
> *And of the temple, "Your foundation will be laid."*

Here we have a specific prophecy that refers to a particular man named Cyrus, yet the prophecy was recorded about 150 years before Cyrus was even born. Not only that, but the prophecy predicts the rebuilding of Jerusalem and the temple at a time when they were still standing. This would be like me saying on August 11, 2001, "Of the World Trade Center, it will be rebuilt." You'd think me crazy! Yet it wasn't until a hundred years after Isaiah's prophecy that Jerusalem and the temple were destroyed. King Nebuchadnezzar took care of that in 586 B.C. However, after the Persians conquered the region in 539 B.C., Cyrus, king of Persia, as recorded in Ezra chapter 1, made his proclamation for the Jewish exiles to return and "rebuild the house of the LORD... in Jerusalem."

Fascinating. Cyrus did exactly what the Lord said he would do. Again, Cyrus's actions were foretold 150 years before the man was even born. "The LORD of hosts has sworn, saying, 'Surely, just as I have intended so it has happened, and just as I have planned so it will stand.' "[10] Therefore, "Many plans are in a man's heart, but the counsel of the LORD will stand."[11]

Every prophecy in the Bible regarding the past, right up until today, has come true—approximately 2000 of them. No human being in history, from before the time of Nostradamus to Jeane Dixon and beyond, has been able to make predictions with 100-percent accuracy. And, unlike the Psychic Hot Line, the Bible needs no disclaimers regarding the accuracy of its prophecies. You will never find the small print "for entertainment purposes only" under the biblical prophetic writings.

The wonderful thing is that since every prophetic word has been fulfilled in the past, every word God declared concerning this time forward will also take place. I cannot help but recall Jesus' words in Matthew 5:18: "Truly I say to you, until heaven and earth pass away, not the smallest letter or stroke shall pass from the Law until all is accomplished"—which leads us to our next segment.

The Word on The Word

If the Scriptures were a bit suspect, I think you could safely conclude that Jesus' use or quotation of them would certainly express His views on them. It seems obvious to me that Jesus viewed the Scriptures as authoritative, since He confirmed their validity, referred individuals to them, quoted them when facing His greatest enemy, and rebuked the Pharisees for treating their traditions with higher esteem than the Scriptures.[12] In John 10:35, Jesus said that "the Scripture cannot be broken," and He also claimed to be the fulfillment of them. Now, one would assume that since He believed Himself the fulfillment of them, He would have to regard them as authoritative. Consider Jesus' words in the following passages:

- *To Satan in Matthew 4:4,7,10:* "It is written, 'Man shall not live on bread alone, but on every word that proceeds out of the mouth of God.'"

    "It is written, 'You shall not put the Lord your God to the test.'"

    "Go, Satan! For it is written, 'You shall worship the Lord your God, and serve Him only.'"

- *To the Pharisees in Mark 7:6-8:* "Rightly did Isaiah prophesy of you hypocrites, as it is written: 'This people honors Me with their lips, but their heart is far away from Me. But in vain do they worship Me, teaching as doctrines the precepts of men.' Neglecting the commandment of God, you hold to the tradition of men."

- *To the rich young ruler in Luke 18:20:* "You know the commandments, 'Do not commit adultery, do not murder, do not steal, do not bear false witness, honor your father and mother.' "

- *To the crowds in John 7:38:* "He who believes in Me, as the Scripture said, 'From his innermost being shall flow rivers of living water.'"

It only makes sense that Jesus viewed the Word of God as authoritative—after all, He is the Word made flesh. "In the beginning was the Word, and the Word was with God, and the Word was God."[13] (I'll share a bit more on this in chapter 7.)

So Much More Than *Life's Little Instruction Book*

The manuscript evidence, the internal evidence such as the fulfilled prophecies and eyewitness accounts, and the external evidence such as history and archeology have all proved the validity of the Scriptures. However, unlike any other writing, ancient or otherwise, it is a living document, and its impact is supernatural. Anyone sincerely desiring a relationship with the living God will find Him by searching the Scriptures. As you know, what I am referring to is not

simply a warm, fuzzy feeling that's fleeting, but an abiding relationship with the Word made flesh.

Isn't it a shame that so many people turn to their Bible as they
would to a "Magic Eight Ball"? Have you ever seen those silly things?
A former co-worker of mine in sales used to keep one on her desk. If
a deal wasn't working out quite right she would shake the little ball
and flip it over to see her answer float to the top. Most of the time it
read, "Try again later." Just as frivolous is the approach some professing believers take to the Scriptures. They flip through it with eyes
closed, and wherever their finger lands, that must be God's will for the
day. God wants His Word to be so much more than that in our lives
because it *is* so much more.

The apostle Paul, in what was his final letter before he was
beheaded, passionately reminded the young pastor Timothy of the
vital importance of Scripture in his life. Even though we know these
things, it is so good to be reminded, isn't it?

> *You, however, continue in the things you have learned and
> become convinced of, knowing from whom you have learned
> them, and that from childhood you have known the sacred writ-
> ings which are able to give you the wisdom that leads to salva-
> tion through faith which is in Christ Jesus. All Scripture is
> inspired by God and profitable for teaching, for reproof, for
> correction, for training in righteousness; so that the man of God
> may be adequate, equipped for every good work.*[14]

The Bible helps us discover the living God and reveals just how we
can enter into an abiding relationship with our heavenly Father. The
Bible also encourages us in our walk with our Lord and painfully
convicts us when we meander off that narrow path. Have you ever
noticed that? Isn't it funny how, at those times when we know we are
out of His will, certain passages in the Bible are the last thing we want
to read? Hebrews 4:12 tells us why: "For the word of God is living and
active and sharper than any two-edged sword, and piercing as far as
the division of soul and spirit, of both joints and marrow, and able to
judge the thoughts and intentions of the heart." That's deep stuff—no
wonder so many people become inflamed when we quote it!

From the Scriptures, we can discern truth from error, like the Bereans, who offer a great example of how we are to do just that. "The brethren immediately sent Paul and Silas away by night to Berea, and when they arrived, they went into the synagogue of the Jews. Now these were more noble-minded [intellectually honest I'd say] than those in Thessalonica, for they received the word with great eagerness, *examining the Scriptures daily to see whether these things were so.*"[15] Also along these lines we are told to "be diligent to present yourself approved to God as a workman who does not need to be ashamed, *handling accurately the word of truth.*"[16] In other words...no "Magic Eight Ball" approach to the Scriptures. Since it is a living document, our approach should be with prayer and "great eagerness." This implies an expectant heart listening for the heart of God. Isn't it just magnificent that God has given us such an incredible gift?

Final Thoughts

As a mom, wouldn't it be foolish for me to have my children memorize verses from a collection of books that are not what they claim to be? Wouldn't it seem like a waste of time to study that collection of books if they were only filled with myths and legends? Wouldn't it seem silly to trust that same collection of books as a roadmap for this present life and the next if they weren't authoritative? The wonderful news is that the Holy Bible is what it claims to be. It is indeed the inspired Word of God.

What I've shared in this chapter regarding the reliability of the Holy Bible is not new information—and there is so much more I wish I could say here. However, at the end of this chapter (and of each chapter in this book) you will find a list of suggested resources. My hope is that you will try to get ahold of some of these wonderful books, because they will serve you well in answering any further questions that may arise regarding the validity of the Holy Bible and many other concerns.

For far too long, I think, we've been uneasy about defending the Holy Bible against objections. Some of them sound so convincing. But take heart and don't take it personally if someone snickers at your love of the Word. Keep in mind that anyone's quarrel with the reliability of the Holy Bible is not with the one who honors it as such, but with the One who provided it for any person who desires a love relationship with the Almighty. Jot down your seeking friend or relative's concern if you are unsure about an answer. If you can't find the answer in this simple guide to reasons for faith, you will most certainly find the answer in my suggested resources. Also, keep in mind that just because you aren't sure of an answer, that does not mean there isn't one available. God has already seen to it.

My dear sister, there is no doubt about it—you can trust the Holy Bible because it is divinely inspired, historically reliable, indestructible, infallible, and life-changing. So go right ahead and pick one up at a nightstand near you—and feel confident to encourage someone you know to do the same.

Questions for Reflection

1. *Is relying on the Bible like relying on the last person in the "telephone game"? Why or why not?*

2. *Can you name three things that make the Bible unique?*

3. *What makes the Bible much more than a mere instruction book?*

4. *Have you ever read your Bible cover to cover?*

5. *Have you considered visiting Tyre for your next vacation?*

Suggested Resources

When Critics Ask: A Popular Handbook on Bible Difficulties by Norman Geisler and Thomas Howe. Baker Books, 1992.

I'm Glad You Asked by Kenneth Boa and Larry Moody. Cook Communications Ministries, 1995.

The New Inductive Study Bible: Discovering the Truth for Yourself. Precept Ministries International. Harvest House Publishers, 2000.

CHAPTER 2

Belief in God's Existence

he existence of God—quite an overwhelming subject to ponder, isn't it? At one time in my life, even the thought was a bit too overwhelming. I must admit that for about ten years I was among those who questioned God's existence. And even if He did exist, I imagined Him as aloof as ever to my personal circumstances. Clearly, God had other things to occupy His time, like keeping the universe running, rather than concerning Himself with what concerned me.

I suppose this is why I have great empathy for those who struggle in this area—because I know that not all individuals who classify themselves as atheists or skeptics are in fact hostile to the idea of God's existence. I meet many individuals who are as I once was: I was frustrated that, while intellectually I could recognize the evidence, yet when it came to trust and faith, for me it was not a leap into the Everlasting Arms but seemed more like falling headlong into a dark, bottomless chasm. Still, as I think back on those years of doubt, I suspect that the Lord was calling out to me all the while, as in the old Dr. Seuss story *Horton Hears a Who,* "I am here! I am here! I am here!"

"Are You there, God?" It is indeed the human heart's deepest longing. How wonderful that when our hearts cry toward heaven, He readily replies, "Of course I am." To earnestly seek the answer to the question of God's existence is a worthy pursuit, since the Scriptures state that "without faith it is impossible to please Him, for he who comes to God *must believe that He is,* and that He is a rewarder of those who seek Him."[1] It is God's greatest desire that we know, not only that He is, but that He loves us and longs to bless us. After all, He said, "I have loved you with an everlasting love; therefore I have drawn you with lovingkindness."[2] He also knows that some of us need a bit more help in the *drawing* process because, more often than not, the rejoinder is, "If God is really there, if He really exists, why doesn't He *show* Himself?" He has certainly done that, and in some rather obvious ways. Perhaps that's why so many people miss Him.

The psalmist wrote, "The fool has said in his heart, 'There is no God.'"[3] Aside from the fact that there is ample evidence for God's existence, I imagine what is so foolish about the unbeliever's disbelief is that to say with perfect confidence *there is no God* that person would have to possess the attributes of omniscience and omnipresence. The foolish unbeliever would have to know every nook and cranny in the universe and would have to dwell *in* every nook and cranny to make sure God wasn't lurking behind some supernova in an attempt to hide. However, if the unbeliever did possess the attributes of omniscience and omnipresence, he would *be* God. Thus his argument against God's existence would be self-refuting, in that God would be asserting that God does not exist!

Perhaps, since belief in God is quite intuitive, you long ago recognized the folly of the atheist. However, when it comes to articulating reasons why you believe God exists, you'd simply like to share something a bit more concrete than personal intuition. The purpose of this chapter is to guide you in doing just that. Before I present several tests for the existence of God, there are a couple of challenges to belief that I'd like to talk about since they seem to be pretty popular among unbelievers. Once I've addressed these concerns and posed three basic tests, I'd then like to show you that the "God of the tests" and the God of the Bible are indeed one and the same.

Santa Claus, Dark Chocolate, and Wishful Thinking

I think we have all encountered individuals who attempt to suppress a hearty chuckle at our profound belief in God. For them, the notion of an eternal Being whose power is as unlimited as His presence and knowledge seems too fantastic to be true. Perhaps the idea of such a Being should be reserved for a child's bedtime story. They seem to discount God's existence and the validity of even asking the question because they view belief as mere wishful thinking. God is simply an imaginary Santa Claus reserved for gullible believers to lean upon when the rigors of life seem too much to bear. However, wishful thinking does not prove or disprove the existence of God.

Think of it this way. Imagine, for example, that because of your extraordinary gardening abilities, you have been invited to speak at your local garden party's yearly luncheon. It is a spectacular event. Since your nerves seem to be getting the better of you, you rush off to the restroom as quickly as possible just before you are introduced. Knowing time is short, you leap out of the bathroom stall, turn on the faucet to wash your hands—and lo and behold, the water shoots out of the faucet with blinding speed, ricochets off the porcelain sink, and soaks the front of your dress. Panicked, you attempt to dry it with a paper towel...only to find that hundreds of teeny-tiny white balls are now plastered to the front of the beautiful sapphire-blue material. Suddenly, you hear the hostess make an announcement. You realize you have just been introduced. You quickly leave the restroom and move as swiftly as possible to the lectern, hoping no one will notice the huge wet spot and paper-towel lint all over the front of your new dress. But alas, you can hear the muffled snickers from all around the room.

Still maintaining your composure, you smile graciously and comment lightly, "It's just water—it'll dry soon, I'm sure," while gently brushing off the front of your dress. Just then, Mrs. Snodgrass, the senior executive administrative director of the garden club, steps behind you, cups her hand over the microphone, and whispers in your ear. You're horrified by her words—you had no idea that you'd inadvertently tucked the back of your dress into your pantyhose before your hasty exit from the bathroom stall. And unfortunately, this is the best thing that happens to you all day.

Now imagine further that later on, as soon as you enter the front door of your home, dejected and humiliated, you throw yourself onto your couch and wishfully think about or desire a large box of dark chocolates. Your plan is to eat the entire box as fast as possible. After all, everyone knows that, next to ketchup, dark chocolate is *the* comfort food. Now, the simple fact that you desire a large box of dark chocolates, or wishfully think about it, does not mean there is no such thing as dark chocolates. Wishing for, or hoping for, or desiring something to exist does not disprove its existence.

When applying this to God, we can take it one step further. The fact that human beings share a deep-seated need for God actually *confirms* His existence, in that we only desire or need that which actually exists.

When I was pregnant with my son, my deep-seated need wasn't for dark chocolate. What I craved—and will tell you without a moment's hesitation, *needed*—(though much to the chagrin of my poor husband, who tried not to watch me eating them) were anchovies delicately wrapped around little green capers. Good stuff. My craving, my desire, my deep longing was for something that actually existed— namely, anchovies delicately wrapped around little green capers. Such is our need for the existence of God. We hunger for what exists, not what doesn't—otherwise, how would we know to hunger for it? This consuming need for God is an ingrained aspect of the human condition...and on a global scale, no less. Now that's what I call a craving!

You're in Good Company

Similar to the "wishful thinking" camp of individuals are those who think belief in the existence of God is simply anti-intellectual. Personally, I think this is a rather poor excuse to abandon the topic. Besides, as far as the intelligence test goes, believers are in pretty good company. Perhaps you are familiar with Francis Bacon, Blaise Pascal, and Sir Isaac Newton, the latter considered by many to be the greatest scientist who ever lived. The renowned physicist Michael Faraday, Gregory Mendel, Louis Pasteur, the famous archaeologist William Ramsay—and one of my favorites, who produced hundreds of uses for the peanut, George Washington Carver—all had an abiding faith in and held a biblical worldview about the existence of God.[4]

Now, lest I be misunderstood, I do not name these brilliant individuals in order to show that belief in God is not anti-intellectual and thus prove God's existence. Personally, I am of the opinion that, if what a simpleton believes in is actually the truth, then no matter what the subject, that's all that should really matter to any of us. *Truth* is our measuring rod, not those who recognize that truth...or those who we think it would be kind of cool to identify with.

The "You Started It First" Test

Have you ever been asked the question, "Mom, where did I come from?" For me, up until recently the answer "California" sufficed. Since we moved to Washington state from the San Francisco Bay area when our daughter was just nine months old, that answer seemed safe enough, and it satisfied her curiosity. However, someday I know that the question will take on an all-new dimension. "Where did I come from?" might well turn into "Where did California come from?" and to "Where did this planet come from?" and to—you guessed it— "Where did the universe come from?" I think it's a pretty valid question. After all, if the universe does exist, where *did* it come from? What caused it? Thankfully, there really are only a few options.

1. It's an Illusion

I wrote, "*if* the universe exists" because perhaps, just perhaps, the universe is merely an illusion—something I created in my mind. But, even to have a mind to ponder these heady things, I must myself exist—and since I am not floating around in nothingness, what I experience around me must also exist. You are reading my book, correct? At the very least the two of us exist! I think if we keep going along on this course it could quite possibly lead to silliness at best, madness at worst. It reminds me of a telephone conversation I once had with a woman who was convinced I didn't really exist. When she asked me to prove my existence to her, I simply replied, "You're talking to me." (Actually, I didn't feel too insulted, since she was convinced she didn't really exist either!)

Obviously, we know the universe is not an illusion because certain events are predictable. For example, my desk calendar notes when full moons will occur. From this invaluable information I can then plan those wonderful evening marshmallow roasts in the backyard with the family. Since an illusion exists only in the mind of the one suffering from it, the company that made my calendar would also have to be suffering from the same illusion as the astronomers and us, the marshmallow-roasters. Therefore, I think it is safe to conclude that the universe is not an illusion.

2. It's Always Been Here

Our next option is that the universe is eternal. It has simply always existed. Herein lies what I believe is yet another self-evident concept, one that even small children can recognize. Simply listen to them arguing on a playground:

"*You* started it first."

"No, *you* started it."

And so it goes, back and forth. Why? Because everyone knows that everything and everybody had a beginning, from quarrels on a playground to the grandeur of the universe.

Aside from the fact that this notion of a beginning point is intuitive, we can see that everything around us is running down and wearing out. Therefore, it *must* have had a beginning. Just to prove wrong a high-school science teacher who once wrote on a progress report to my parents, "Judy never, NO NEVER, pays attention," I do remember learning about the second law of thermodynamics. This law states that our universe and everything in it is running out of energy, is wearing down, and is subject to decay. If the second law of thermodynamics weren't a reality, Pluto would not be encased in ice, and Estée Lauder wouldn't be making a fortune from Advanced Night Repair, Resilience Lift, Fruition Extra Multi-Action Complex, and Idealist Skin Refinisher facial product sales. Therefore, the universe is not eternal. It had a beginning.

3. It Came from Nowhere

Another option is that the universe suddenly emerged from nothing. However, I also remember—just to greatly encourage that wonderful science teacher who was so concerned about my limited attention span—that from nothing, nothing comes. Every cause has an effect. Just as one of those children on that playground caused the argument, so also the universe is the effect of a cause.

4. It Has a Cause

Since the universe is not an illusion, nor is it eternal, nor could it have emerged from nothing, I think our final option is the most reasonable one. Something independent of the universe had to cause it to come into being. Something beyond or greater than the universe had to cause its existence. The universe could not have caused itself. It could not have brought itself into being. After all, it wasn't there to bring about its existence.

I think that the answer lies not in *what* caused the universe but *Who* caused it. Obviously, what we observe are the effects of an eternal, uncaused First Cause of everything—an omniscient (all-knowing), omnipotent (all-powerful), omnipresent (everywhere-present) Being who transcends (is above and independent of) the material universe.

In a nutshell, the universe was brought into existence at a certain moment in time from nothing (no pre-existing material) by the power of an eternal, ultradimensional, creative, relational Being, who brought it about expressly for the purpose of having a love relationship with those He created in His image. (I'll share a bit more on that later.)

Now, though I don't think it would occur to my daughter, knowing my son, it is highly probable that one day he will move beyond the question "Where did the universe come from?" to "Where did God come from?" or "Who created God?" Actually, if God were created He would not be God, since one of God's greatest attributes is that He is eternal. If another God had created Him, He would not be eternal. Rather, He would be only immortal, and thus finite, or limited, by virtue of the fact that He had a beginning. Nevertheless, as Mikael's mommy, I do feel compelled to offer a response just in case he brings up the question. So here goes: "Mikael, even if God had been created by His God, it really wouldn't make much difference. Because He is our Creator, we are accountable and answerable to Him alone."

I guess we can think of it this way. Try as they might, my children can appeal to their grandparents for that extra scoop of ice cream, but the decision rests with my husband and me. We are their final authority as their—for lack of a better term—"creator." Therefore, their appeals to Grammy and Pop Pop are futile. As their "creator" we shall exercise our authority, and our answer is, "No, six scoops of double-chocolate-chip mint ice cream should be plenty!"

The Billboard Test

A couple of very dear friends of mine, who I've been sharing the gospel with for as long as I have known them, told me of an incident that happened to them as they were driving home to Washington state from Idaho. In an attempt to test the validity of my claims that God exists, while traveling along in their car they began calling out, "God, if You're *really* out there, show us a sign!" Just then, they noticed a huge billboard reading,

YOU WANTED A SIGN?
HERE IT IS.
GOD.

They were stunned. Now, you may think their experience just a funny coincidence. But when we discussed the cause of the cosmos by an uncaused First Cause (there's a mouthful!), I used the words *creative* and *relational* to describe God. I also said He created us for a love relationship—that this vast universe was created for the purpose of His having a love relationship with those He created in His image. If this is true, two things should follow:

1. The billboard "sign" was not just a funny coincidence.

2. Neither is the universe and all it contains.

The Sign

There are certain aspects, aside from the obvious, that I think are worthy to consider when contemplating my friends' billboard "sign." I believe it just might help us to recognize other "signs" that answer the question of God's existence and also confirm His particular interest in human beings. Think, for a moment, about the following aspects of the "God" billboard.

1. The letters were not scattered all over the poster board haphazardly.

2. The letters were neatly centered in three rows.

3. The letters were written with a particular font and style.

4. The letters were written in a certain order and the order formed words.

5. The punctuation and spelling of those words were correct.

6. The words conveyed a message.

Upon seeing such a sight, my friends' next question would be the same question we would ask, I'd imagine. Obviously, we would wonder who put it there, or who wrote it. The reason we would wonder *who* and not *what* is that the sign conveys a message. The message communicates an idea. We say *who* because the sign has a purpose. Its purpose is to convey the message that God will respond when asked to do so. The sign speaks of *design*. The sign has purpose and meaning, which means that there is a mind behind the design— a rational, intelligent, thinking mind that wishes to communicate a vital message to individuals who can respond. It is the same with God's universe.

The Design: Made for a Reason

> *When I consider Your heavens, the work of Your fingers,*
> *The moon and the stars, which You have ordained;*
> *What is man that You take thought of him,*
> *And the son of man that You care for him?*[5]

The interesting thing about this passage of Scripture is that, immediately after a consideration of the heavenly bodies, the psalmist, in a state of awe, realizes that God made them spectacular for a particular reason. The psalmist believes that God made them with humankind in mind. I think this passage of Scripture is a beautiful reminder that God made the heavenly bodies exquisite so human beings could gaze upon them and be brought to a place of worship, not of the created, but of the Creator.

"The heavens declare the glory of God; and the firmament showeth His handiwork."[6] "Handiwork" directs us to a *Handiworker*.

There is a reason why modern science was born out of a Christian worldview. Since a rational, intelligent, orderly Being created the universe, scientists recognized that the universe and all it contains could be observed, tested, and verified. Kepler, the man considered to be the founder of physical astronomy, summed up the whole matter quite nicely when he stressed that he was simply "thinking God's thoughts after Him." At this point, let's consider God's creation as a whole, looking for a sign of His existence or His handiwork.

There are two important questions to answer:

1. Does the universe show any signs of design, thus proving the existence of an Intelligent Designer?

2. Is there any evidence that would lead us to conclude that the Mind behind the design "cares" or "takes thought of" human beings in particular, as the above Psalm mentions?

The Design: Made Just for Us

I believe that both of those questions are sufficiently answered by what is referred to as the *anthropic principle*. Oh, don't let that term frighten you. Patrick Glynn, in his book *God: The Evidence*, explains the principle in a nutshell:

> The anthropic principle says that all the seemingly arbitrary and unrelated constants in physics have one strange thing in common—these are precisely the values you need if you want to have a universe capable of producing life. In essence, the anthropic principle came down to the observation that all the myriad laws of physics were fine-tuned from the very beginning of the universe for the creation of man—that the universe we inhabit appeared to be expressly designed for the emergence of human beings.[7]

What are some of these constants and values that must be precise for human life and on earth specifically? The following barely scratches the surface:

• Oxygen comprises 21 percent of the atmosphere. If it were 25 percent, fires would erupt. If 15 percent, human beings would suffocate.

- If the gravitational force were altered by only 1 part in 100,000,000,000,000,000,000,000,000,000,000,000,000,000 (that should be 41 zeros), the sun would not exist, and our beautiful moon would either crash into the earth or sheer off into space.

- Further, even a slight increase in the force of gravity would result in all the stars being much more massive than our sun, with the effect that the sun would burn too rapidly and erratically to sustain life.

- If the centrifugal force of planetary movements did not precisely balance the gravitational forces, nothing could be held in orbit around the sun.

- If the universe were expanding at a rate one-millionth—think about that—just one-millionth slower, the temperature on earth would be 10,000° C. (Never mind your sunscreen.)

- Even a slight variation in the speed of light would alter the other constants of physics and prevent the possibility of life on earth. (Currently the speed of light is defined as 299,792,458 miles per second.)

- If Jupiter were not in its current orbit, our humble planet would be bombarded with space material. Jupiter's gravitational field acts as a cosmic vacuum cleaner, attracting asteroids and comets that would otherwise strike earth.

- If the thickness of the earth's crust were greater, too much oxygen would be transferred to the crust to support life. If it were thinner, volcanic and tectonic activity would make life untenable.

- If the rotation of the earth took longer than 24 hours, temperature differences would be too great between night and day. If the rotational period were shorter, atmospheric wind velocities would be too great.

- If the axial tilt of the earth were slightly altered, surface temperature differences would be too great to sustain life.[8]

(So much for *random chance*...but more on that in chapter 5.) This mind-spinning information is not a recent discovery. In 1973, the established astrophysicist and cosmologist Brandon Carter presented a major thesis before the world's most renowned "scientific minds of our time." Apparently heads are still reeling over his paper, entitled "Large Number Coincidences and the Anthropic Principle in Cosmology." Coincidences? All one has to do is consider the intricacies of the human body, or even a bug for that matter, to recognize that there had to have been a Mind behind the design. The anthropic principle, I think, reveals that as far as that Mind making accommodation for a creature, human beings were it. Now don't you feel special?

The Fred C. Dobbs Test

Are you like me in that you enjoy old movies? I'm not talking about the '70s. I mean films that were made in the '30s, '40s, and '50s. I really appreciate them—and *The Treasure of the Sierra Madre* is one of my favorites. In this dramatic 1948 film Humphrey Bogart plays a hobo, Fred C. Dobbs, who turns to gold prospecting along with a fellow down-and-outer. At the beginning of their adventure Dobbs is shocked at even the suggestion that greed might get the better of him, but unfortunately, it surely does...along with intense paranoia.

Toward the end of the movie, Dobbs (Bogart's character), viewing his companion as a rival, shoots his innocent former friend. Believing he has killed the man, the prospector throws the gun down and leaves the scene of the crime. What happens next is fascinating. Dobbs, now alone in the middle of the night and the middle of the wilderness, trying to comfort himself, lies beside the campfire and begins to mutter nervously, "Conscience, what a thing. If you believe you got a conscience it'll pester you to death. But, if you don't believe you got one, what could it do to you? It makes me sick, all this talk and fussing about nonsense." Just then, he rests his head on his arm, closes his eyes as if to sleep—and not a moment later, opens them very wide as he stares with a horrified expression into the roaring campfire right before his face.

This leads us to the third test for the existence of God. Bogart's character, Fred C. Dobbs, could not escape the turmoil within his soul no matter how hard he tried to talk himself out of it. Though some individuals vigorously wish to escape any acknowledgment of God, they cannot escape their innate sense of right and wrong, guilt, and impending judgment. This notion, this thing within us that C.S. Lewis referred to as our sense of *oughtness*, is experienced in all cultures, through all ages, among all human beings.

But where did it come from? Where did this innate sense of self-evident right and wrong come from? Why would you experience a sinking feeling if you slipped into someone's long-awaited parking space during the Christmas rush? It's not illegal—and if might makes right, perhaps the Volkswagen Beetle driver should freely give the parking space to you since you drive a gas-guzzling, environmentally abusive nine-person SUV. Yet you would experience a bit of inner turmoil and thus would proceed to do one of four things: 1) Condone it. "Perhaps I shouldn't have done that, but I just had to…I'm in a terrible hurry." 2) Call it justice. "That always happens to me—it's about time I did it to someone else." 3) Deny it. "I did *not* take her spot, she was waiting for one further down." 4) Own up to it. "Oh my—I'm so sorry. I *know* it was wrong of me to do that. Here—I'll back out right away."

Now, why even think twice about that situation? Is this sense of right and wrong—this feeling of justice or injustice that leads each of us to condone, justify, deny, or confess—simply our personal opinion, or is it just possible that we intuitively appeal to a greater Authority outside or beyond ourselves? The answer can only be that this special thing within human beings that's known as the conscience or the moral law, this universal feeling we experience, is a gift bestowed upon us by a moral Lawgiver.

Is the moral law unique to humans? Yes. Fido the family dog is not burdened with guilt because he ate the family's roast. Fido does not go before the family and say, "I've sinned. Forgive me, for not only have I eaten the roast, but I have wrongly accused Bootsy the cat!"

Dolphins, after killing one of their own for sport (as has recently been discovered they do), do not gather a group of their dolphin peers to conduct a trial. The accused does not bear remorse and seek redemption for its soul or reconciliation with the bereaved dolphin family.

Yes, every human being—and only human beings—recognize the moral law. It is evident within, or self-evident, as Romans 2:14-15 clearly states: "When Gentiles who do not have the Law do instinctively the things of the Law, these, not having the Law, are a law to themselves, in that they show the work of the Law written in their hearts, *their conscience bearing witness, and their thoughts alternately accusing or else defending them.*

Guilt: It's a Good Thing

Now, you may be wondering why on earth I would refer to the conscience as a gift from God. Truly, the moral law, when followed, is a blessing to humanity. At the very heart of the moral law is the commandment to love God above all else, and to love our neighbor as we do ourselves. When we deny that spiritual check in our conscience, we do harm to others and to ourselves. However, when we respond to that God-given burning in our conscience and obey our internal conviction, the product is an individual with self-restraint. And the Golden Rule is then lived out in shoe leather.

If we feel guilt, why do we feel it? To attempt to talk ourselves out of its existence, as many do with the existence of God, just ignores the question. Obviously our conscience is there for our spiritual survival, just like our fight-or-flight response is there for our physical survival.

Think of it this way. If what restrains me from picking your pocket is the fact that I might get caught, what will I do when no one is looking? But if what restrains me from picking your pocket is the moral compass within my heart that tells me it's wrong, if my reason is that I don't wish to hurt the heart of the One to whom I owe thanks and praise, then my life will be a blessing to others and I will have peace in my soul. Therefore, guilt is indeed a blessing to humanity. Unfortunately, all too many individuals in our society suppress their moral compass, that feeling of guilt that implies an impending judgment. If only they would allow the moral law to lead them to the moral Lawgiver who put it there in the first place—for just such a purpose!

Comparing the God of the Bible to the God of the Tests

Wow, God is a big subject! I think the best thing to do at this juncture, for simplicity's sake, is take a look at the points we've covered in the previous sections and see how they correlate to the God of the Bible. Since we've established the fact that the Bible is divinely inspired, we can certainly trust it to give an accurate description of the One who provided it. This will give us an opportunity to make that correlation. For not only is the Bible's message consistent from Genesis to Revelation in regard to God's redemption for mankind, but it is also consistent regarding the attributes and character of the God of the universe, of intelligent design, and of the moral law.

The God of the Bible Is the God of the Universe

Since we know there are certain attributes that the God of the Bible would have to possess in order to cause the existence of the universe, we'll turn to the Scriptures to find those unique characteristics. In Exodus 3:14 God told Moses, "I AM WHO I AM." He did not say, "I once was…" or "Someday, I sure hope to be…" but, "I AM WHO I AM." In other words, the God of the Bible has always existed. He is eternal. The God of the Bible also brought everything into existence out of nothing and sustains His creation as well:

- *Genesis 1:1.* "In the beginning God created the heavens and the earth."

- *Colossians 1:17.* "He is before all things, and in Him all things hold together."

- *Hebrews 1:3.* "[He] upholds all things by the word of His power."

- *Acts 17:25.* "He Himself gives to all people life and breath and all things."

The God of the Bible, the uncaused First Cause of the universe, never needs a nap! While we might need our three-o'clock doze, His unlimited power never wanes or diminishes, according to Isaiah 40:28:

> *Do you not know? Have you not heard?*
> *The Everlasting God, the* LORD,
> *the Creator of the ends of the earth*
> *Does not become weary or tired.*

The God of the Bible is clearly the cause of our existence as well, as stated in Isaiah 44:24-25:

> *Thus says the* LORD, *your Redeemer, and* the one who
>   formed you from the womb,
> *"I, the* LORD, *am the* maker of all things,
> *Stretching out the heavens by Myself*
> *And spreading out the earth all alone,*
> *Causing the omens of boasters to fail,*
> *Making fools out of diviners,*
> *Causing wise men to draw back*
> *And turning their knowledge into foolishness.*

The God of the Bible Is the God of Design

Indeed, the God of the Bible has caused the universe, including this planet, to have a "love relationship" with the creatures He created in His image. Verses 18 and 12 of Isaiah 45 are wonderful pictures of the anthropic principle, I believe:

> *Thus says the* LORD, *who created the heavens*
> *(He is the God who formed the earth and made it,*
> *He established it and did not create it a waste place,*
> *But formed it to be inhabited),*
> *"I am the* LORD, *and there is none else."*
> ..."It is I who made the earth, and created man upon it.
> *I stretched out the heavens with My hands,*
> *And I ordained all their host."*

Again, God created all things and upholds all things in order to have a love relationship with those He created in His image. His desire is an abiding relationship with the people who will respond to Him in pure love and worship, offering Him the praise that is due to Him. "Worthy are You, our Lord and our God, to receive glory and honor and power; for You created all things, and because of Your will they existed, and were created."[9]

The God of the Bible Is the God of the Moral Law

Certainly, the God of the Bible set a standard for morality. What we recognize intuitively as right and wrong is perfectly consistent with His standard, and there are no contradictions. The Bible reminds us that we do indeed possess an internal witness of the law, that human beings "show the work of the Law written in their hearts, their conscience bearing witness and their thoughts alternately accusing or else defending them."[10]

Prophecy and the God of the Bible

Thankfully, there can be no doubt about it—the God of the Bible *is* God. While fulfilled prophecy is a great piece of evidence to establish the validity of the Bible, God tells us that the real purpose of prophecy is to prove He is the one and only true and living God. Since He is the God who caused this humble planet's existence, He is also sovereign over it, and thus He can predict what happens on it. In Isaiah 44:7-8 God declares there is no God besides Him and offers a challenge to any so-called god. You would imagine that the challenge still stands:

> *Who is like Me? Let him proclaim and declare it;*
> *Yes, let him recount it to Me in order,*
> *From the time that I established the ancient nation.*
> *And let them declare to them the things that are coming*
> *And the events that are going to take place.*
> *Do not tremble and do not be afraid;*
> *Have I not long since announced it to you and declared it?*
> *And you are My witnesses.*
> *Is there any God besides Me,*
> *Or is there any other Rock?*
> *I know of none.*

All I can say to that is…neither do I.

Final Thoughts

As I mentioned earlier, my heart certainly goes out to those who honestly struggle with the question of God's existence. I'm sure you too have a heart for those who struggle with this subject, so may I make a few suggestions? The next time you are with your honest skeptic friend who doubts the existence of God, perhaps over a nice hot cup of mint mocha you just might want to pose this question: "Do you think it is possible that the God who created us would like us to know He exists?" If she is truly intellectually honest, her reply will be "Yes." The reason why she will answer "yes" is that God has placed in every human heart the recognition of His existence. Since she can agree that His existence is at least possible, you can then present to her some of the tests for His existence. I think Romans 1:19-20 confirms and sums up the tests quite nicely:

> That which is known about God is evident within them; for God made it evident to them. For since the creation of the world His invisible attributes, His eternal power and divine nature, have been clearly seen, being understood through what has been made, so that they are without excuse.

As He does for each and every one of us, God reveals Himself in a variety of ways so that your doubting Thomasina may know Him— no excuses. Your loving witness is just one of the many ways.

Again, I think it all boils down to intellectual honesty. Simply remind your friend of Deuteronomy 4:29: "Seek the LORD your God, and you will find Him if you search for Him with all your heart and all your soul." If your friend is serious about her search for the answer to the question of God's existence, He will surely answer her. That's His promise.

Questions for Reflection

1. *What is the folly of the atheist?*

2. *How can we know that the universe has a Creator?*

3. *Can you explain the anthropic principle?*

4. *Is the conscience simply a matter of feelings? Explain.*

5. *Have you ever tried anchovies delicately wrapped around little green capers?*

Suggested Resources

Mere Christianity by C.S. Lewis. HarperCollins Publishers, 2001.

The Knowledge of the Holy by A.W. Tozer. HarperSanFrancisco, 1998.

A Shattered Visage: The Real Face of Atheism by Ravi Zacharias. Baker Books, 1993.

CHAPTER 3

Faith in Spite
of Popular Objections

*ave you ever noticed how ingrained it is in the human condition to find excuses for just about everything? Sometimes, when we have to, we can sure think quickly on our feet. Someone recently sent me a humorous e-mail suggesting a variety of things for an employee to say if the boss catches her sleeping on the job. (Thankfully, if I need a couple of winks all I have to do is give the kids a quiet project, grab my snuggly blanket, and nestle in on the couch for a 15-minute power nap.) Nevertheless, there they were at my disposal: excuses I could use just in case Jeff walked into the office and caught me drooling on my computer's keyboard. The suggestions ranged from "Oh, I must have made decaf by mistake" to the employee lifting her head as she offers a solemn "In Jesus' name, amen."

Now, if excuses abound for use in the case of an unexpected visit from the boss, how much more for avoiding an encounter with the God and Judge of the universe? Keep this in mind if, when sharing your faith, you become frustrated because so often one objection after another seems like an excuse for holding God at arm's length. Sometimes, some of the more popular objections that unbelievers offer are not really excuses at all, but are actually obstacles to belief for them. How nice it is that we can offer sound answers to the variety of popular objections that we so often hear from seekers!

In this chapter I would like to cover just a few of these objections, including the idea that Christianity is oppressive to women, the charge that the church is filled with hypocrisy, the claim that the Christian worldview is too narrow, and a few others. My hope is that when you hear these popular objections, you will know how to address them appropriately and lovingly—not treating them simply as excuses, but as perhaps thistles surrounding a rose.

Oppression

When I was about 20 years old and lived in the desert, enduring 110° heat for two long summers, I found that oppressive. When I drove from appointment to appointment in bumper-to-bumper traffic all around the San Francisco Bay area as a corporate salesperson, I found that oppressive. When I felt I had no control over my life and carried the weight of every burden upon my shoulders, from finances to diminishing hopes of ever having a child, I found that oppressive. When I would lie in my bed at night, unable to sleep because of a nagging fear of death, I found that to be especially oppressive.

However, when I gave my life to the Lord Jesus Christ, I did not gain mounting oppression, but freedom, a future, and a hope—and so did you. Isn't it sad that many people who look on from the outside assume that Christianity must be terribly oppressive for women? However, this is simply not the case. Oppression is a state of the mind and the soul. Webster defines the word *oppression* in a couple of ways: 1) "unjust or cruel exercise of authority or power," and 2) "a sense of being weighed down in body or mind." It defines the word *oppressive* as "overwhelming or depressing to the spirit or senses."

Words like *weaker vessel*, or *submit* and *submission*, seem to provoke a variety of false impressions for women who have never had this objection properly addressed. Thus, as the serpent beguiled Eve, he has convinced many women in our society that a relationship with Jesus Christ means a life of oppression, of being under the cruel thumb of some male authority figure in the church, or a tyrannical husband in the home, or both. Yet nothing could be further from the truth for godly men and women who truly love and serve the Lord according to His design.

Insult or Compliment?

The phrase "weaker vessel" from 1 Peter 3:7 can conjure up all sorts of negative reactions, which is really a shame. It is unfortunate that many individuals remember two words from the Scriptures yet forget or have never investigated how the words are used.

I must admit, in this day and age the term "weaker vessel" can sound sort of like a slam. However, the reference was not meant to imply that women are somehow inferior to men in some way—rather that as women, we can view ourselves as 24-karat gold, which is delicate, beautiful, and valuable—unlike, say, a steel reinforcing bar.

Perhaps the best thing to do is to look at the use of the phrase in context. Were women perceived by the author as common, inexpensive, disposable metal…or pure gold to be cherished? Peter commands, "Husbands likewise, live with your wives in an understanding way, as with a weaker vessel, since she is a woman; and grant her honor as a fellow heir of the grace of life, so that your prayers may not be hindered."[1]

What a wonderful passage to show our value to God and our position in the Christian faith. Clearly, this passage establishes our equality with men in the kingdom since women are referred to as "*fellow heirs* of the grace of life." But, did you notice that if the husband does not grant his spouse honor as a fellow heir, God will not hear his prayers? It seems to me that the heat is clearly on the guys in this passage.

Chaos or Balance?

Then there's that wonderful word *submit*. With only part of the story, women can take the view that the husband's foot is firmly planted upon the wife's neck. With such a perception of Christianity, no wonder many women feel uncomfortable with the concept of submission. However, to understand this word fully, we must keep in mind that the God we serve is a God of order. One gander at the creation and anyone can see this is true. The universe is not chaotic—it is, in fact, meticulously balanced and orderly. It is the same in marriage. Each member of the family holds a particular level of authority, or headship, in order for there to be order in the home. The word *submit* as used in the Scriptures literally means *to place under in an orderly fashion*. The word has nothing to do with value, but rather with who is accountable for what. If the husband perverts this design by abusing his position or headship in the home, God will hold him accountable for it.

The interesting thing is that everyone submits to someone whether they agree with the Scriptures or not. When I was in the workforce I submitted to the authority of my manager, yet it did not change my intrinsic value as a human being. When I travel, I submit to the authority of the airport security. Yet my intrinsic value remains the same. It is the same way in marriage. God, in His infinite wisdom, called the wife to submit to the authority of her husband. The husband honors the wife as a fellow heir, and the wife honors the husband by submitting to his leadership. (Frankly, I find it quite handy to say on occasion, "Wait till your father gets home.")

Honor and Blessing

Submission is not an insult to women—it is necessary for order. The order was not created by man, but by God. Here again, we must turn to the Scriptures to understand the concept of submission in its proper context. Ephesians 5:22-25 reads,

> *Wives, be subject [submit] to your own husbands, as to the Lord. For the husband is the head of the wife, as Christ also is the head of the church, He Himself being the Savior of the body. But as the church is subject to Christ, so also the wives ought to be to their husbands in everything.*
>
> *Husbands, love your wives, just as Christ also loved the church and gave Himself up for her.*

It really is a beautiful picture. When godly submission is understood and put into action, truly there is harmony in the home. The husband expresses sacrificial love, to the point of death if need be, and the wife responds by submitting to his loving and godly leadership. If the wife happens to be married to an unbeliever, her loving obedience to his authority serves as a testimony. I have seen this repeatedly with women who gave their lives to Christ before their husbands came to the Lord. What usually happens is that the husband will begin to ask his wife to pray about various things. He sees her godly attitude. He watches her prayers being honored. He recognizes a supernatural life change—and it cuts him to the quick. Whether it takes a husband 6 months or 60 years to submit to God, as women we have the ability to bring blessing to the home by our obedience to God and His design.

How sad it is that instead of obeying God's design and plan for marriage, so many men in our culture have become passive in the home as their wives usurp their authority. I don't know which came first in abandoning the God-given role—the passive, disinterested chicken or the hard-boiled egg—but our society is certainly hurting because of it. Especially the children. I imagine it began in the garden, since the Scriptures state that Adam was with Eve when she ate the fruit. And it seems that, without a word, he allowed her to serve him a little forbidden fruit on the half shell.

The truth of the matter is that we are all to submit to one another. The apostle Paul states in Romans 12:10 that we are literally to outdo one another in showing honor. And the Scriptures clearly state the equality of every believer. Paul, who has been accused by some of being a male chauvinist, wrote that "there is neither Jew nor Greek, there is neither slave nor free man, there is neither male nor female; for you are all one in Christ Jesus. And if you belong to Christ, then you are Abraham's descendants, heirs according to promise."[2]

I think it is also important to note that even in the Trinity, though each Person is co-equal, there is headship. The role of the Holy Spirit is to bring glory to the Son, and the role of the Son is to bring glory to the heavenly Father. What is really at the heart of the human objection to submission, whether we are conscious of it or not, is our ingrained bent toward rebellion. It's just that simple.

Real Women's Lib

Has the sexual revolution liberated women…or subjected them to utter horror and bondage? Not long ago I was on a date night with my husband, and we decided to stop for some ice cream while at a large shopping mall in Portland, Oregon. As I was trying to decide which flavor looked the tastiest, I heard a graceful voice ask, "Have you decided yet?" I looked up to see a beautiful young woman whose face was mutilated—yes, mutilated—by nose-piercing, eyebrow-piercing, and lip-piercing. I was so heartbroken for this girl. What bondage! All I could keep thinking from that point on was just how much Satan must hate us. Yet so many are buying the lie.

To know that women who have bought the lie have actually been devastated, all you have to do is look at the effects of the increases of sexually transmitted diseases—and the sterility and death rates for women from these diseases. The painful truth is this: The more that women believe they are liberated from what is referred to as "traditional roles," the more harm they've done to themselves and their children. Since 1993 I have been working with women in women's ministries all across this country. To hear their stories and see the statistics has been heartbreaking. With the legalization of abortion, many women began to view it as almost a rite of passage. But they now carry scars on their hearts and bodies from a choice too painful for me to imagine. Yet now God has called many of these dear women out of bondage, so they can lead others to the same freedom, forgiveness, and future in Christ that they themselves have found.

True women's liberation is only found at the foot of the cross. A perusal of the Scriptures reveals the fact that a woman, in the eyes of the Lord, was just as valuable as any man. For instance, Jesus did not shy away from the Samaritan woman at the well, engaging her in conversation. Though it was taboo in the culture for a Jewish man to speak to a woman, let alone a Samaritan, Jesus offered her an opportunity to receive eternal life. Not only this, but He chose to reveal to her His identity: the fact that He was the Messiah. By her testimony, she was able to reach her community, and many people received salvation.

It was not a group of men who first discovered the empty tomb. It was not a man who first fell at the feet of the resurrected Lord. God used the testimony of women to first proclaim His glorious resurrection. In Acts 18:26, we see that God used Priscilla as teacher to Apollos right along with her husband, Aquila. And in 2 Timothy 1:5, the apostle Paul credited young pastor Timothy's mother, Eunice, and grandmother, Lois, for the fact that the young man had a "sincere faith."

Value, Not Oppression

Truly, wherever the influence of Christianity has spread it has brought freedom and blessing for women. For example, some cultures have viewed women as simply the property of their husbands. Before Christian missionaries came to India, a widow was burned along with her deceased husband whether she wanted to join him in death or not. Tossing infant girls into the sea was also a common occurrence in India up until the nineteenth century, when Christian missionaries were able to bring this horrific practice to a halt. Before the influence of Christianity, in Africa, as in India, wives and concubines were killed upon the death of their chieftains.

There can be no doubt that women owe a debt of gratitude to the influence of Christianity and the value it places not only on women, but on all human life. This is because the Christian worldview acknowledges all human beings as created in the image of a holy God. Christianity is anything but oppressive to women, especially since its Scriptures declare all men and women co-equal before the Father, joint heirs with the Lord Jesus Christ.

Hypocrisy

One of the more popular reasons why unbelievers tend to back away from an invitation to the next potluck seems to be their feeling that they'd rather not associate with the hypocrites. Apparently, for those who raise this objection, the church is filled with them. I must admit that this would make it seem like a rather unpleasant place to spend a Sunday morning if that was my perception.

Usually, when presented with the objection of hypocrisy in the church, I just keep digging. I continue to ask the *why* questions. I find that with certain objections a painful story comes hand in hand. If I take the time, and my acquaintance knows I love her, she will feel safe enough to share a painful story regarding some preacher, priest, or parent who was less than Christlike. I always try my best to validate feelings, especially since this objection can be quite delicate. Nevertheless, there is an answer.

Since so many people regard Jesus as a good, moral teacher, I usually ask, "Was Jesus Christ a hypocrite? Did Jesus just talk about the exemplary life but portray something else, or was His life consistent with what He taught?" I have yet to hear anyone say they believe Jesus is a hypocrite. After all, even unbelieving Pilate said, "I find no fault in this Man." Obviously, Jesus Christ was not a hypocrite— however, fallen individuals who profess to know Him most certainly can appear to be.

Keep Their Eyes on Jesus

It is unfortunate that people will look at struggling Christians as their example of godly living, rather than at Jesus Christ, who is our supreme example. I think it is important to point out that everyone has areas of hypocrisy in their lives—including the folks who raise this objection. It appears to me that people who believe it is wrong to steal seem to have no problem pilfering supplies from the office, placing telephone calls on company lines or time, or mailing their Christmas packages through the company's mailroom. I will never forget, as a rookie sales representative many years ago, how the other sales reps instructed me to figure my mileage for my expense reports. I think the formula went something like this: mileage x 2 + 10. It was very important that they show me the formula. After all, how would it look if my trip to San Jose was 30 miles when everyone else's was 70?

Again, the important thing is to direct attention to Jesus as our example, not to the fallen individuals who profess to know Him. Jesus said in Matthew 7:21, "Not everyone who says to Me, 'Lord, Lord,' will enter the kingdom of heaven, *but he who does the will of My Father who is in heaven will enter.*" Jesus knew there would be those folks who would call upon Him, yet their hearts would be somewhere else.

Remember, walking through the doors of a beauty salon does not make you a manicurist. Sitting behind the little table and shaking the nail polish does not make you a manicurist. Taking money as you sit behind the little table does not make you a manicurist. You could even attempt to do someone's nails, but as soon as you did, unless you actually were a manicurist, your sin would find you out. You would be a hypocrite. The word *hypocrite* as used in the Scriptures can quite literally be defined by the word *counterfeit.*

Therefore, some folks who walk through the doors of their local fellowship are not there because they have an abiding love for the Lord, but rather because they enjoy the social aspect. Some folks pop in on a Sunday because their family attended that church for years. Perhaps you've met folks who have a network marketing business and just want to make their business grow. Then, when everyone they can pitch is pitched, the family suddenly moves to a new church down the road. However, none of these scenarios has much to do with the Lord Jesus Christ and those who truly believe.

Since Jesus addressed the hypocritical religious leaders of His day, He will most certainly address the hypocrites of our day. A perusal of Matthew 23 will give you a good idea of what Jesus thought of counterfeits in the meeting. Since all judgments belong to the Lord, perhaps those who hold this objection should leave it to Him to separate the wheat from the chaff.

Let Sin Abound so Grace May Abound?

Sometimes there can be a little confusion in the mind of the unbeliever about what is actually hypocrisy. Smoking is always a good example because many unbelievers tend to have this innate feeling that the habit of smoking is a sin. Actually, *anything* that keeps us in bondage is sin. Anything that controls us more than the Spirit of the Lord is sin. However, what an unbelieving onlooker does not understand is that that woman who just put out her cigarette before walking into the church hall was recently freed from the bondage of drunkenness. What they don't know is that the Lord is currently working on her habitual lying, and with great success. Yet some people look on and say, "What a hypocrite—telling me there is freedom in Christ and then lighting up her cigarette." Oh, that we would all be as perfect as those who judge unjustly. Thank the Lord we aren't, because the sad fact is, those who judge in this manner do not see their own hypocrisy.

Truly, the woman with the cigarette can proclaim freedom in Christ. How wonderful it is that the Lord is patient with us. Now, what *would* make the smoker a hypocrite is if she rebuked the unbeliever for smoking then sneaked behind the bushes to light up her own in the hope that no one would notice.

However, the fact remains that all of us sin. Each one of us falls short of God's holy standard. The good news is that we don't have to carry the shame, the guilt, or the penalty of our sins. Yes, we do suffer the consequences of our sin, but isn't it wonderful that when we confess, He is faithful and just to cleanse us of all unrighteousness? Now, this does not mean we can sin with reckless abandon in one moment and then turn around and confess in the next, only to willfully start the cycle all over again. God will not tolerate constant willful sin. Since true believers are children of God, He will discipline them. "You have forgotten the exhortation which is addressed to you as sons, 'My son, do not regard lightly the discipline of the Lord, nor faint when you are reproved by Him; for those whom the Lord loves He disciplines, and He scourges every son whom He receives.'"[3]

As believers, we really can't get away with much, can we? Our hearts grieve when we grieve the heart of God. Our confession is a product of sorrow over the transgression, not a means of getting the slate clean only to dirty it again willfully.

Here Today, Gone Tomorrow

Under the umbrella of "hypocrisy" is the objection that many followers of the Lord Jesus Christ eventually fall away from that faith. If Christianity is so freeing and wonderful and promises a new life, why do so many turn away from the faith?

I think this is best answered by 1 John 2:19: "They went out from us, but they were not really of us; for if they had been of us, they would have remained with us; but they went out, so that it would be shown that they all are not of us." If folks fall away from the faith, the faith they had was not genuine in the first place. The fact that they left is proof positive they never were regenerated in Christ, they never were new creations, or born again, to begin with. The parable Jesus told in Luke 8:11-15 regarding the different ways individuals hear the Word and react is a perfect picture of how some people can look good at first, but wither away in short order. Some fall away due to their lusts, their fears, life's pleasures, or the enemy of their soul, while others grow and are fruitful for the kingdom.

Unfortunately, there will always be wolves among the sheep. Oh, how folks love to remind us of those who have had to confess some horrible transgression over the television or radio. How quick the unbeliever is to use these examples as proof that Christianity doesn't really work, because if it did, these things would never happen.

Yes, we must grant that there are indeed wolves among the sheep, but we can also point out that many more individuals haven't fallen from grace as those public figures have. Many more perform selfless acts for those who are suffering and are in need. For example, we have missionary friends who minister in China, and we have others in the Sudan, whose newsletter every month brings me to the point of tears. Many more truly faithful Christians open hospitals and schools, feed the hungry and house the homeless, clothe the naked and care for the orphan.

These faithful believers far outnumber those who begrudgingly confess to some scandalous transgression. They bear fruit and their fruit remains. We know them by the fruit they produce. Again, you cannot look to the individual as an example of how we ought to be, because we are bound to our flesh until the Lord takes us to glory. Our only example should be the Lord Jesus Christ and, as the Scriptures state, "He who believes in Him will not be disappointed."[4]

Environment

Some people find it hard to believe that we would follow Christ for any other reason than that we were born into a Christian environment. Their thinking is that our faith only goes as deep as our generations. They think that because a parent believed, we simply followed in their belief.

However, when talking with many professing Christians I find that their backgrounds are quite varied. Not all believers come to Christ from homes that truly trusted and believed in the Lord. For example, I know of a woman who grew up in the Jewish tradition and converted to Catholicism. She then married a man who had grown up Catholic, then had later rejected Catholicism to become a pantheist. Though they raised their three children in the Roman Catholic tradition, they were weaned spiritually on the occult. They were introduced to and dabbled in everything from the Ouija board to tarot cards to visiting fortune-tellers. Of those three, each rejected Catholicism, and two radically gave their lives to the Lord Jesus Christ later in life. The third child continues to dabble in the occult but, as she puts it, "just for fun."

The point is that individuals come to Christ not because of upbringing or environment. Otherwise, we would sure have a hard time explaining the number of radical Muslims in Sudan who give their hearts to Jesus Christ, as reported by our missionary friends. We would also have a hard time explaining the growth of Christianity in places like China or the former Soviet Union. Obviously, a relationship with Christ is not based upon environment.

Nonetheless, if my children, who are growing up in a Christian environment, maintain their passion for the Lord, that certainly will not invalidate their faith. My parents taught me well that if I did not look both ways before crossing the street, I would become part of the pavement. As an adult I did not dismiss this claim, because I found it to be a valid one. It is not that we believe because our parents would be displeased if we rejected the faith, or that we are somehow conditioned or brainwashed into believing. The reason why we believe is that we have found the claims of Christ to be true.

People are not born Christians. To be sure, they could have been born into a Christian home or environment, but Christianity is a decision. It is a conscious choice made by an individual who understands the consequences of accepting or rejecting Jesus Christ. Quite simply, Christianity is a decision of the will, not a result of pressure from parents. Otherwise, you'd probably see what I addressed in the previous section entitled "Here Today, Gone Tomorrow."

Too Narrow Is the Gate?

Imagine for a moment that it is Christmastime. Fudge is in the air. You decide to surprise the kiddies by making chocolate–marshmallow turtles. Upon opening your cookbook, you suddenly feel indignant. *Surely there must be a better way of making these turtles—this recipe is entirely too narrow,* you think. Instead of using the narrow suggestion of two cups of semisweet chocolate chips, you decide to use four-and-a-half cups. Instead of the narrow suggestion of two tablespoons of vegetable shortening, you decide (because, after all, you want to keep your girlish figure) that one teaspoon of shortening should be just fine. And because the children enjoy them so much, you are going to use 30 large marshmallows instead of the narrow suggestion of 12. And, as far as that cup of pecan halves goes, you feel that Rice Krispies are far better. Now, following this type of thinking, how do you think your turtles will turn out?

If there are hazards in rejecting a recipe because it seems too narrow, how much more so with eternal matters? Obviously, the question isn't one of narrowness but reasonableness of belief. Narrowness does not govern whether something is right or wrong. Narrowness can't be a way to determine what's true. If, by following the prescribed method, we arrive at the correct conclusion, who cares if the method is narrow?

Still, this is an extremely popular objection. Christianity seems too narrow. I think many feel this way because the Christian proclaims that Jesus is the only way to salvation. However, the misunderstanding comes when folks think we proclaim this out of our own imagination. Indeed Christianity is narrow, but not because the Christian proclaims it—rather, because Jesus Christ did. In Matthew 7:13 Jesus said, "Enter through the narrow gate; for the gate is wide and the way is broad that leads to destruction, and many are those who enter through it. For the gate is small and the way is narrow that leads to life, and there are few who find it."

Light for Those Who Haven't Heard

I think it is wonderful when an unbeliever suddenly has a heart for people who have never heard the gospel. All right, perhaps I am being a bit facetious—because we know this objection has little to do with a desire to see others come to faith in Christ. Rather, it has everything to do with a false view of God. The unbeliever's basis for rejecting Christianity is the idea that God will send people to hell because they haven't had a chance to believe and receive, and therefore God is unjust. How can God send people to hell simply because they haven't heard? However, the fact is, He doesn't.

Thankfully, God holds us accountable only for what we do know, not what we don't. If anyone on this planet, no matter where he or she is, truly seeks to have a relationship with the living God based on the light God has given them, He will reveal Himself to them. He will not reject them.

If an individual you are talking with raises this objection, simply remind her of this wonderful truth: God has ordained that she live in a land where access to the gospel is abundant, through Christian fellowships, bookstores, and radio. Suggest that because she has such access, perhaps the Lord will use her to communicate the gospel to other people groups, since her heart is so tender toward them. Really, though, the question is not about folks in other lands. Rather, with such an abundance of knowledge in *her* land, why is *she* still rejecting?

Imagine you are drowning, when suddenly a lifeboat floats in front of you. The captain of the lifeboat reaches out his hand to draw you into the boat, but you reply, "No, thank you. I will not come into the boat and be saved, because in another land there is an individual drowning who has not yet heard about this boat of salvation." Little do you realize that while you drown, the person you are so concerned about in the other land has grabbed onto a piece of wood left by the captain of your lifeboat. Though it is not the entire lifeboat, the person has found salvation by it nonetheless. The same captain that could save you has saved the foreigner while you choose to drown.

Hellfire, Brimstone—and a Party?

Finally, I would like to address a rather popular objection that actually makes the hair on the back of my neck stand on end whenever I encounter it. I have friends—perhaps you do, too—who think they'd rather not go to heaven because they'll miss the party with their friends in hell. I find this attitude particularly frightening because it is obvious they have no clue about the reality of eternal torment.

I think it is important to remember that since God is holy, every sin is a violation against God. God is also just and cannot allow sin to go unpunished. Since all human beings sin because of our fallen nature, we are all justly condemned to hell. However, since God is also a God of infinite love and mercy, He sent His Son to take the penalty for our sin onto Himself. We therefore have an opportunity to receive eternal life with God rather than eternal judgment in hell. Jesus Christ made a way of escape, through faith and belief in Him alone.

Thus, God does not send anyone to hell—rather, we are condemned to hell by virtue of the fact that we sin. Anyone who finds himself or herself in hell is there because he or she made the choice to reject God's method of salvation. God has provided every opportunity to help humanity avoid making that choice. He has made Himself known through the light of creation, the light of conscience, the light of Himself coming into a lost world, and the light of His Word—*so that we are without excuse.*

When speaking of hell, Jesus often referred to it as *Gehenna,* a real place that was familiar to those He was speaking to. I imagine He referred to hell as Gehenna so the people who were listening to Him would have some frame of reference. I like how Ralph Muncaster explains this place called Gehenna:

> Gehenna is an actual place in the Hinnom Valley just southwest of Jerusalem. Solomon, in his later years, turned the valley from a natural paradise into a place where the idols of his wives' pagan gods were worshiped. Infants were sacrificed into terrifying flames. The valley later became the city cesspool where refuse, dead animals, and bodies of criminals were dumped and burned. Worms ate into dead flesh until they were consumed by the blaze. The fires never ceased. The foul stench never stopped. To the Jews, Gehenna was absolute hell.[5]

Hell, originally created for Satan and his minions, is far from a wild party where a bunch of pagans happily thumb their noses at God. Revelation 19:20 speaks of it as a "lake of fire which burns with brimstone [sulphurous flames]." Now, if you've ever smelled rotten eggs, you've had a whiff of the scent of brimstone.

Hell is also described in Matthew 8:12 as a place of "outer darkness." When I think of "outer darkness" I imagine the lava caves beneath the ground near Mount St. Helens, not far from my home. When you hike through the caves, guides strongly suggest, you should make sure you have at least two sources of light. Not long ago a friend of mine who is a youth pastor took a group of teens into the caves. They hiked as far as they could go—then the entire group turned off all flashlights and lanterns. His goal was to give the young people a sense of what the outer darkness of hell might feel like. Most of the teens told me that after just a few seconds they felt disoriented, paranoid—and yes, very frightened. Their lights didn't stay out for long. However, the outer darkness of hell is complete and eternal. Hell is also a place of abject loneliness, since in outer darkness you cannot be comforted by the sight of a friendly, compassionate face.

Matthew 8:12 also speaks of hell as a place of "weeping and gnashing of teeth." Have you ever been in so much pain that you actually gnashed your teeth? I have. When I was in my early 20s I accidentally, while quickly removing my contact lenses, tore the corneas on both of my eyes. It was horrible. I cannot not imagine that pain for all eternity.

According to Mark 9:48, hell is also a place where the "worm does not die, and the fire is not quenched." If the worm does not die, neither do the beings who exist there.

Hell is a horror. It is a place of eternal torment with Satan, demons, and worms, with weeping and gnashing of teeth, with disorienting and frightening darkness and unquenchable fire that reeks of rotten eggs. Yet the greatest horror of hell is total separation from not only loved ones and friends, but from God for all eternity—forever remembering the willful rejection of the light God gave. Some party, huh?

Final Thoughts

At the beginning of this chapter, I suggested that seekers who offer one objection after another should not be misinterpreted as simply offering excuses. Rather, with love and patience we should address each one of their objections. However, it is indeed possible that some unbelievers will continue to pose objection after objection simply to avoid the heart of the matter. I call these "encounters with a 'yeah, but.'" If you have ever been involved in a counseling ministry you've probably met a "yeah, but." No matter how many objections you satisfactorily answer, their reply is, "Yeah, but what about…"—and off they go with yet another objection. I'd like to suggest a handy way of getting around the perpetual "yeah, but" challenge. (This is something I also suggest in my communication training manual *A Time to Speak*.[6])

If you sense that the objection could be an excuse to stave off conversion, simply ask straightforwardly, "Other than your concern that Christianity seems oppressive to women, is there anything else you can think of that would prevent you from placing your trust and faith in Jesus Christ right now?"

In all honesty, there is no objection on earth that needs to be answered to allow someone to come to know the Lord. Salvation comes by an act of the will prompted by the Holy Spirit, not by answering objections. However, having answers to popular objections does help to remove obstacles to conversion, or help ground believers in their faith. This is the ministry of Christian apologetics. My prayer for you is that, after understanding these answers to some of the more popular objections, you will feel better equipped when chatting with a seeker you would just love to see in the kingdom.

Questions for Reflection

1. *How would you address the perception that Christianity is oppressive to women?*

2. *What should you do to eliminate areas of hypocrisy in your life?*

3. *Who was it that said the way to salvation is narrow?*

4. *What is the worst aspect of hell?*

5. *How long was it, after you read the segment on Christianity being narrow, until you made chocolate–marshmallow turtles?*

Suggested Resources

What If Jesus Had Never Been Born? by D. James Kennedy and Jerry Newcombe. Thomas Nelson Publishers, 1997.

Her Choice to Heal by Sydna Masse and Joan Phillips. Scripture Press Publishers, Inc., 1998.

How Should We Then Live? by Francis A. Schaeffer. Crossway Books, 1983.

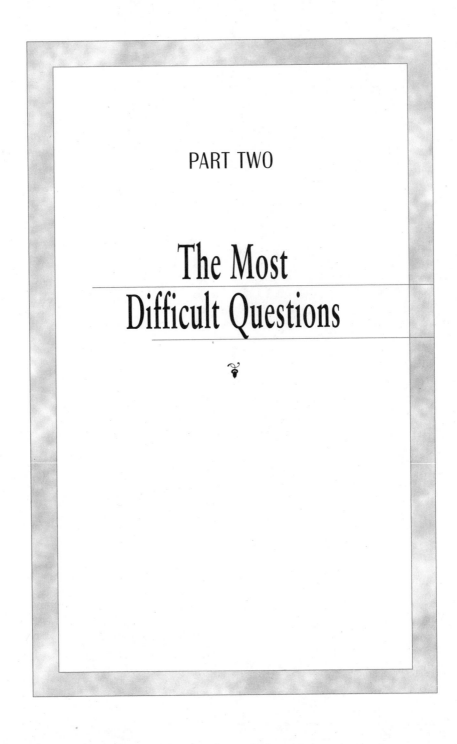

PART TWO

The Most
Difficult Questions

CHAPTER 4

Confidence That Truth
and Moral Absolutes Matter

I hope you will grant me a little license to describe a familiar scene from chapter 18 of the Gospel of John. Here's how I picture what the situation might have been like. I imagine it a terribly somber moment. Pilate was in a pickle. He knew that the Person standing before him was completely innocent...then again, there's the crowd to please. Frustrated, Pilate almost pleads with Jesus to tell him of His crime, so that he can have his cause for sentencing this Man the Jewish leaders have brought before him.

Pilate had asked the Jews plainly, "What accusation do you bring against this Man?" Did they give a clear-cut list of offenses? Were the supposed offenses so outrageous that Jesus was deserving of death? Their response to Pilate was weak and vague: "If this Man were not an evildoer, we would not have delivered Him to you." In other words, "Surely you can't possibly imagine that we, the religious leaders and pillars of the community, would deliver up to you an innocent man, can you?"

After a short dialogue, Pilate asked Jesus, with dire exasperation in his voice, "What have You done?" Jesus proceeded to tell him of His kingdom. Pilate then blurted out, "So You are a king?"

Jesus responded calmly and directly. "You say correctly that I am a king. For this I have been born, and for this I have come into the world, to testify to the truth. Everyone who is of the truth hears My voice."

Pilate, knowing the Man before him was innocent, yet knowing the consequences of not keeping the political situation favorable, in an almost discouraged state muttered, "What is truth?"...and never waited for an answer.

What a missed opportunity. There Pilate stood—before the embodiment of truth, before the One who could give him the answer that really mattered...and he didn't bother to stick around long enough to hear it. Pilate had searched for the truth: "What accusation do you bring against this Man?" "What have You done?" "So You are a king?" To each of these questions he waited for an answer, yet when he finally asked the most important one, he chose to answer it himself... and only with another question.

I think there are many individuals right under our noses who, like Pilate, mutter to themselves, *What is truth?* Though they desperately desire the answer, believing in their heart there is no such reality as truth they attempt to develop their own. However, for whatever reason God has chosen to reveal the truth to you and me. On what basis God chose us, only He knows, but for what purpose, we surely know. Truth was not revealed to us so we could keep it a secret. It was revealed to us so that we might share it with others. But today that is certainly a challenge. This is why I thought that a discussion on truth—what it is, what it isn't, how we can spot it and test it, and why it matters—just might help further ground you in the truth, and hopefully help you lead many others to the Truth as well.

What Is Truth?

Let's take a moment to look at two basic types of truth: 1) *subjective* truth, and 2) *objective* truth.

1. The Reference Is to a *Subject*

Subjective-truth claims have to do with the subject, namely the person who is making the claim. For example, if I told you that olive green is the most beautiful color, or that brisk autumn mornings feel better than warm summer evenings, or that Cheez Doodles always taste great with peanut butter on them, you can consider all of these to be subjective-truth claims. Subjective-truth claims are an internal kind of truth.

You really can't test the validity of a subjective-truth claim other than by the claim itself—and by the fact that you might witness me wearing olive green while taking a stroll every brisk autumn morning, smiling away as I munch on Cheez Doodles dipped in peanut butter. Now, you might trust my claim, but your proof from observing my dress and actions might also be mistaken. I might really dislike olive green but have just happened upon a wonderful sale at Wal-Mart. Autumn mornings may be the only time I ever have an opportunity to go for a stroll…and as for my unusual snack, I just might be pregnant.

2. The Reference Is to an *Object*

Objective-truth claims are quite a bit different than subjective-truth claims. Objective truth is true whether anyone wishes to believe it true or not. One truth claim has to do with personal preference, taste, or opinion (that's why you really can't test the validity of subjective truth). The other truth claim concerns an object apart from the individual.

For instance, imagine that you and I are sitting in my dining room enjoying a spot of tea together. You notice my matryoshka dolls—nesting dolls—in my curio cabinet. You ask where I purchased them, and I tell you I bought them while in Russia. Suddenly you begin to eyeball me because you're not quite sure you want to accept my claim that I visited Russia. (Now, I know you're not really like this. You know I wouldn't lie to you—but let's just say, for example…) Because you're not convinced just by my claim, I begin to show you proof that I was, in fact, in Russia. I might show you photographs or a video taken of me while I was there. I might also produce my passport or the stub of my plane ticket—destination, Khabarovsk. I just might call other individuals who were also on that trip as witnesses that I was indeed in Russia. The point is, I can prove I was actually there. Now, you might still be skeptical—but the fact remains, whether you wish to believe it or not, I did go on a missionary trip to Russia. That is objectively true—true whether you wish to accept the claim and the evidence or not.

A chair is a chair, and while I might like to express my subjective opinion by calling it a table, my opinion is not rooted and grounded in objective truth. I can call it what I like or believe whatever I wish, but the fact remains, it's still a chair.

Unfortunately, what has happened in our culture—and in others as well—is that in the mind of many, objective truth no longer exists. All truth is subjective, especially in moral or spiritual matters. Truth is simply relative to each individual's personal taste or opinion. However, what seems to have escaped the notice of those who hold to a worldview that there is no objective truth, is that this worldview still assumes one very foundational truth. That one truth is the truth that there is no truth to know. In other words, to say, "there is no truth," is a truth claim about truth...which those who hold this position say no one can know. Oops. Their argument against truth is self-refuting, which is to say, their claim against truth breaks down as soon as they make the claim. If there is no truth, their position can't be true either.

Nobility in Neutrality?

Many individuals who hold to a relativistic moral and spiritual worldview, actually feel that this is a neutral position—because, for them, every person's worldview is just as valid as the next. As the thinking goes, since all individuals should accept everyone's brand of faith as equally valid, moral relativists can view themselves as "nobly neutral." Therefore, it only makes sense that they rebuke Christians for "pushing" their morality or spirituality on others since to the relativist, spirituality, morality, and truth are simply matters of personal taste or opinion. In other words, "How dare Christians suggest that their view is superior or more accurate than another?" Since all views are equally valid, neutrality is king!

However, since when is it noble to be neutral concerning what is intuitively right or wrong? Would neutrality be noble in our attitude regarding September 11, or the Columbine shootings? Was neutrality noble in Hitler's Germany?

If the goal of moral and spiritual relativism is to silence the gospel, it seems to be working. Many of us are now less apt to share our faith because, after all, who wants to be accused of pushing or imposing morality, or a particular worldview, on others? Yet what many of us Christians in this predicament do not realize is that a worldview has been imposed upon *us*. Namely, that it is wrong for us to impose morality, a certain spirituality, or a certain worldview on others. So the imposition is upon Christians—to remain silent. Telling Christians they should not share the gospel is a worldview that tells them to hush up. Personally, I believe the best thing we can do is lovingly and gently draw the relativist's attention to the inconsistencies of her view, and show her that her view itself is anything but neutral.

Are *Christians* Relativists?

Considering the variety of denominations within Christianity, some might just think the Christian the relativist. However, as we in Christendom know, while we may disagree on nonessential issues, in the essentials of the faith, united we stand! When it comes to the basics, we believe the same things about the nature and the character of God, humanity's fallen state and our inherent sin condition, the virgin birth of Jesus Christ and His sinless life, Jesus' atonement for our sins on the cross, His bodily resurrection, and His imminent return. Christians also agree on other essentials of the faith, as stated in the major creeds of Christendom. So our disagreement over nonessentials like style of worship and music, whether we use wine or grape juice, matzo or pita bread during communion, or whether we sprinkle or dunk 'em during baptism, does not make Christianity somehow just another branch of relativism.

Also, just because Christians have some level of disagreement among themselves does not mean that there is no objective truth within Christianity. Disagreement doesn't prove that one can never arrive at truth. The first question should be, what is the nature of our disagreement? Is it whether or not Jesus Christ was really God in the flesh, or is it over whether the preacher should wear a robe or a jacket and tie?

Healthy disagreements are actually good things because through them is exactly how we arrive at objective truth. We can arrive at truth by working through the most logical and best-supported arguments. Unfortunately, the nobly neutral relativists have many people convinced that to *argue* (I did not say *quarrel*) is bad and that those who engage in argument are simply divisive and annoying. This is why, if you attempt to engage in a constructive dispute that leads to truth, inside or outside of the church, you just might be accused of violating the Rodney King axiom: "Can't we all get along?" However, just because there is disagreement does not mean we can't all get along. Amen?

Do All Roads Really Lead to a Heavenly Home?

Imagine you are traveling by car. You have a particular destination in mind, but it is a glorious day and you feel great, so you decide to take your time. Just then, you happen upon a fork in the road. You stop for a moment, and as you're trying to figure out which road to choose, your driving companion says, "It doesn't really matter which one you take—they all go to the same place." Though you are a bit leery of that claim, her confident air prompts you to comply, so to the right you veer and continue on your journey. Suddenly, the smooth pavement is gone, and you find your car is hitting pothole after pothole. Another fork in the road. You say to your traveling companion, "Perhaps I should just look at the map."

"What for?" she says, confident and carefree. "All these roads lead to our destination. Just pick the one that looks good." Again, you follow her advice...but this time, the ride gets bouncier and you find you are traveling over very rough terrain. Thank goodness you recently put new tires on your Yugo. Another fork. By now, your peace is gone and outright panic is setting in. "This road can't be right," you say to your blissful companion. "Perhaps I should go back. Or perhaps I really need to check the map."

"It wouldn't make any difference. Whatever road we take will lead to our destination. Go ahead and pick the one that feels right to you and press on." Her self-assuredness does give you a bit of comfort. After sitting there for quite some time, you finally choose a path based upon your feelings and not on the map. Aghast, you find that the road you chose has led you to a sheer cliff. As you slowly and carefully attempt to back your car out of this predicament, you notice a sign that reads, "KEEP MOVING FORWARD. DO NOT BACK UP. SEVERE TIRE DAMAGE."

The moral of the story? All roads do not lead to the same destination in the material world or the spiritual. Neither are all religions basically the same, leading everyone to a heavenly home—as some might like to suggest. For example, some world religions are polytheistic. Polytheists worship many different gods, while Christians believe that there is only one true and living God. There are those who believe in cyclic rebirth, or reincarnation, but the Bible states in Hebrews 9:27 that, "It is appointed for men to die once and after this comes judgment." Though members of other world religions feel that their good works or deeds will save them, the message of the gospel is that we are saved by grace alone, and this is a gift from God. And since the religions of the world tend to contradict each other in some rather significant ways, all world religions are definitely not the same.

Frankly, we aren't the only people of faith who claim a particular spiritual expression is true or the correct path to take. Members of most world religions believe that their religion is *the* one true road to salvation. After all, the reason why homicide bombers or Christian missionaries are willing to lose their lives is because they both hold that what they believe is true. However, if worldviews contradict, the thing to do is not judge them as equally valid simply because their adherents hold the view or are willing to die for it. What makes sense is to test the validity of the claims—to examine them and ask which worldview or system of belief is more reasonable to believe. This is vitally important since the Scripture calls us to "test *and* prove all things [until you can recognize] what is good; [to that] hold fast."[1] The fact that we are instructed to test means that there is a correct answer and that we can find truth and reality regarding spiritual matters.

Sincerely Wrong

Sincerity and passion are wonderful things. However, if they are misguided, the result can lead us off a cliff—or at the very least, to severe tire damage. Many people today sincerely believe that, as long as you are sincere in what you believe, what you believe is sincerely true *for you*. Yet I'm sure you know as well as I that, again, sincerity absent objective truth can be rather costly.

For example, do you remember the seemingly innocuous little cult that called itself "Heaven's Gate"? Certainly this group was extremely sincere about what it believed. So sincere, it was reported that some members apparently felt it necessary to return an expensive telescope, claiming it was defective. The shopkeeper looked it over, then, puzzled, asked the cult members, "Why is it defective?"

Their reply: "One cannot see the UFO [flying behind the Hale-Bopp comet] with it." How terribly tragic that, not long after, 39 cult members were dead, sincerely believing they had to commit suicide in order to board a UFO that could not be seen with *any* telescope. Now, while their sincere intentions were to reach heaven, their method was sincerely...and tragically...wrong.

The Perils of a "Free to Follow Your Own Imagination" Kind of World

If ever a proverb were fitting for a worldview that dismisses objective truth, it has to be Proverbs 16:25:

> *There is a way which* seems right *to a man,*
> *But its end is the way of death.*

At first blush, moral relativism does seem somewhat good, fair, and noble. That's why so many individuals inside the church and outside are taken in by it. But truly, its end is not only intellectual, but also spiritual death. The sad reality is that this thinking has subtly permeated just about every area of our society, and it is currently being foisted upon our children.

Not so subtle was an example of this I found in an article from the September 1998 edition of the *Portland Parent*. Actually, it was my then 5-year-old daughter, Nicole, who spied the rather aloof-looking child on the magazine cover with the title and byline above his head, "'Nurturing a Child's Spirituality' by Gail E. Hudson." As it turned out, the Lord used this article for a precious teaching moment with my daughter as I read it aloud to her over a burger and fries. I never made it very far along before it was time to once again ask, "Nicole, does that make sense?" At five years old, ya know...it pretty much doesn't. The following is just an excerpt:

> Once on a walk with my 4-year-old daughter, she turned to me and asked, "What do you think God looks like?"

I pointed to the tufts of grass growing in the cracks of the side-
walk, the towering cedar trees, and the silvery, overcast sky. "I
believe all of this is the face of God," I said reverently.

"Not me," she replied matter-of-factly. "I think God is a woman
with brown hair, a polka-dot dress, and red, bouncy earrings."

Although nothing in my teachings or beliefs had presented God
as a flashy-dressing female, I was soothed by my daughter's vision.
It told me that she felt free to follow her own imagination and create
a personal relationship with God. And more importantly, she was
uninhibited by my own or anyone else's spiritual images and
mandates. As a parent trying to nurture my young daughter's innate
spirituality, I figured that I must have been doing something right.

First of all, don't you just want to give this little girl a hug? How
wonderful that, though distorted, her thoughts are about God! It's
funny, isn't it, that this precious little girl attempted to make the case
to her mother about what God looks like, and very "matter-of-factly,"
I might add.

However, I don't know about you, but I'm not so sure I'd be
soothed by the description. Personally, my immediate question would
be to ask my little girl why on earth she envisioned God in such a way
in the first place.

"Inhibitions"?

The author clearly believes that truth concerning spiritual matters
is purely subjective. Mamma thinks it is perfectly fine—and is in fact
soothed by her daughter's image of God as a flashy-dressing female,
while she can see the face of God in tufts of grass, towering trees, and
an overcast sky. No matter, to Mamma both views are equally valid.
And thus Mamma sincerely believes that she must be doing something right. To leave her daughter with an image of God as a flashy-
dressing female is right, to persuade her daughter to share her view of
God is wrong.

Since Mamma holds the worldview that it is wrong to inhibit
her child by imposing her spiritual image or mandate upon her, she
does have some measure of what is right and wrong, or what is true
or untrue, concerning spirituality. Obviously, for Mamma, it is virtu-
ous to allow your child to feel free to follow her own imagination

concerning her view of God, and it is wrong to correct her. Apparently, the best way to nurture the innate spirituality in our children is to leave them to themselves. (Yet I wonder what Mamma's reaction would be if her daughter came home and said, "I know what God looks like—He looks like Jesus Christ because I have come to believe that 'in Him all the fullness of Deity dwells in bodily form.'"[2] We can only hope and pray.)

Isn't it just like the enemy of our soul to try to convince us that the worst thing we can do for our children, when passing on to them our spiritual torch, is to inhibit them by imposing a spiritual mandate or image upon them? But one thing this loving mother did get right. Indeed her daughter does have an innate spirituality. The reason why she does is because a God who is real and knowable put it there...for the very purpose of wooing her into a personal relationship, not with tufts of grass, or trees, or the sky, but with Himself.

Proof of Truth

Can we follow our own imagination concerning reality? Or do we all intuitively recognize that objective and absolute truth exists? Everyone can agree, whether we wish to admit it or not, that there is objective truth in a variety of areas of reality.

Law is one such area. If perhaps, while at a Nordstrom department store, I decide to slip a fancy piece of costume jewelry into my pocket, no doubt I'll feel a tap on my shoulder from security upon my hasty departure from the store. Now, I can talk indignantly until I am blue in the face about how shocked I am that the jewelry somehow got there. Nevertheless, the security camera truthfully caught me red-handed on film. The truth in this case will not set me free but send me off to the county jail.

Mathematics is another area where objective truth is reality. For example, my wonderful husband, Jeff, spent quite a few years as a builder. Imagine for a moment that he applied a relativist worldview to his measurements while framing a home. Can you just see the face of the homeowner as she asks, "What happened to my twelve-foot walls? These are only three feet tall!" To which my husband the relativist builder would reply, "Well, what is twelve to you is three to me!"

Medicine might get a bit sticky for a patient in a world lacking objective truth. Perhaps you thought you were going into the hospital for an appendectomy, but upon awakening in the recovery room, you find that your incision seems to be in an odd place. When you question your doctor, she shares her subjective feeling that, for her, the appendix and gall bladder are basically the same thing. And, don't you dare try to impose your worldview on her!

And, heaven forbid, hair care! What if my hairdresser, for example...oh, I don't even want to go there. I think you get the general idea.

Obviously, the relativist can say whatever she likes about her opinion that objective truth does not exist—however, her language and behavior prove ōtherwise. She approaches her checkbook, the products she buys, and the doctors she visits with the notion that words have a particular meaning and that some very important things in life are just objectively true.

Truth in Morality: It Exists and It Matters

As you can just imagine, the painful and natural outcome for a society that dismisses the reality of objective truth, and especially moral absolutes, is adherence to the idea of doing what is right in your own eyes. After all, who can say anything is wrong? Since many Christians are uncomfortable with just how to confront the politically correct crowd, their silence has allowed this kind of thinking to catch on like wildfire. It is Habakkuk 1:7 right here in our own nation: "They are dreaded and feared. Their justice and authority originate with themselves."

Just to show you how pervasive the worldview of moral relativism is, consider for a moment what the United States Supreme Court stated in 1992 in *Planned Parenthood vs. Casey.* What the U.S. Supreme Court essentially did in this case was to grant credence to the "follow your own imagination" philosophy in some of the most fundamental matters. (Obviously, for the Supreme Court to have come to such a conclusion on the nature of truth and meaning, the groundwork had been laid long beforehand.) Here is just a snippet of the court's opinion:

> Our law affords constitutional protection to personal decisions relating to marriage, procreation, contraception, family relationships, child rearing and education.

The justices then cited a couple of cases and went on:

> These matters, involving the most intimate of personal choices a person may make in a lifetime, choices central to personal dignity and autonomy, are central to the liberty protected by the Fourteenth Amendment. At the heart of liberty is *the right to define one's own concept* of existence, of meaning, of the universe, and the mystery of human life"[3] (emphasis mine).

There it is—Moral Relativism 101, right from the pen of the U.S. Supreme Court. The court's opinion in 1992 was that we no longer need to burden ourselves with the objective truth that personhood affords protection under the Fourteenth Amendment of our constitution. (*Planned Parenthood vs. Casey* spoke of pre-born children, but the door is obviously open to deprive other individuals of "personhood" as well.) No longer need we concern ourselves with being endowed by our Creator with certain inalienable rights. In fact, we can dismiss Him altogether because we, the autonomous individual, can define our own concept of existence, of meaning, of the universe, and of human life. And apparently, we can define what value we place on human life, if we happen to place any value on it at all. This is why we can call them babies if we want to keep them, "products of conception" if we don't. It's our choice. Semantics makes all the difference.

Now, while you may call it murder, the Nazis called it the Final Solution. While you may call it mayhem and horror, Eric Harris and Dylan Klebold called it justice. And do you see how prison almost makes no sense in this sort of world—after all, how dare we impose our morality on others? Frightening, isn't it? Yet there is hope, and wisdom, and freedom. Don't despair—the good news is that you are not in the dark in regard to moral relativism, and the great news is... neither is God.

The Truth Will Set You Free

I know this might seem pretty bold, but it *is* possible to arrive at truth in spiritual matters and thus possess a right view of God and His method of salvation. Thankfully, God has indeed said something about Himself and the way we are to view and approach Him. He has not left our pursuit of Him up to a simple matter of taste or opinion, as you might select your favorite brand of salad dressing.

That He is, *who* He is, and *how* we draw near to Him, are matters of objective truth: truth whether or not anyone wishes to accept or acknowledge it as such. God in His love, and mercy, and grace never meant for those He created in His image to have their own subjective expression of spirituality. Now, I don't know about you, but I praise God for the truth and simplicity of the gospel. "There is salvation in no one else; for there is no other name under heaven that has been given among men by which we must be saved."[4] He, being the perfect heavenly Parent, did not leave His children to themselves—instead, He went to great lengths that they might know truth.

How many of us can attest to the fact that in our fallen, rebellious state we desire always to do our own thing, and especially in our spiritual expression and standards of morality? Romans 1:18 states that our natural inclination is to "suppress the truth in unrighteousness."

Unfortunately, our fallen nature has put us at enmity with God. Our fallen state has left us with the desire to worship because we are spiritual beings, but in our depravity, we seek to replace the true with a counterfeit. If it were not for the gracious beckoning of the Spirit of God that prompts our response, we would each be left in the pitiable state described in Romans 1:21-23:

> *Even though they knew God, they did not honor Him as God or give thanks; but they became futile in their speculations [opinions] and their foolish heart was darkened. Professing to be wise, they became fools, and exchanged the glory of the incorruptible God for an image in the form of corruptible man and of birds and four-footed animals and crawling creatures.*

Our blessed Lord requires that we pursue truth in our approach to and worship of Him. Jesus expressed God's heart and desire for His image-bearers beautifully in His conversation with the Samaritan woman at the well:

> *"An hour is coming, and now is, when the true worshipers will worship the Father in spirit and truth; for such people the*

Father seeks to be His worshipers. God is spirit, and those who worship Him must worship in spirit and truth." The woman said to Him, "I know that Messiah is coming (He who is called Christ); when that One comes, He will declare all things to us." Jesus said to her, "I who speak to you am He."[5]

The Way, and the Truth, and the Life...Truly!

Have you visited your local bookstore lately? If not, pop into one and peruse the books located in the section marked "Spirituality." It's quite an eye-opener. I did this the other day in one of those large national bookstores and purchased a little book that immediately caught my eye. (I managed to get the last one. I'm sure they'll order more since its sales, at this writing, are in the tens of thousands.) The title of the book is *Conversations with God for Teens,* and it's written by Neale Donald Walsch. In this little book geared toward young people, "God" is supposedly answering a teenager's questions. I thought you might like to know what "God" is saying to our young people. The following excerpts are just a taste:

> It may be a surprise for most humans to learn that there is no such thing as right and wrong. There is only what works and what doesn't work, given what it is that you are trying to do.
> ...Absolute Right and Absolute Wrong do not exist. A thing is "wrong" only because you say it is wrong, and a thing is "right" for the same reason.
> ...Right and wrong, therefore, do not exist as absolutes, but only as momentary assessments of What Works and What Doesn't Work. You make these assessments yourself as individuals and as a society, given what you are wishing to experience and how you see yourself in relationship to everything else that is.
> ...In the book *Friendship with God,* I brought the human race a new gospel that would heal the world in two sentences:
> *We are all one.*
> *Ours is not a better way, ours is merely another way.*[6]

Now, you're probably thinking, *Where did he get this stuff to tell our kids?* Well, it didn't start with the United States Supreme Court in 1992, and it didn't start with the New Agers or the postmodernists of today, or even with Neale Donald Walsch. It's original source is pretty obvious—simply put, it comes straight from that old snake in the grass. Of him, Jesus shared this comment: "He was a murderer from the beginning, and does not stand in the truth, because there is no truth in him. Whenever he speaks a lie, he speaks from his own nature, for he is a liar and the father of lies."[7]

Misquoting the One Who Is the Truth

Well, the father of lies is at it again. The serpent of old who's called Satan and the devil doesn't own one original thought, and he often quotes Scripture to prove his case. How sad, though, that many people still fall for it. On page 85 of *Conversations with God for Teens,* a teen questioner, who is astonished to learn that "God" does not judge because nothing is "bad," asks Walsch's caricature of God the following question. Below it, you will find "God's" answer:

> *God does not make judgments? I thought that's what God* did.
> Well, the human race has been thinking that for a long time, but it's not true. It's one of those misunderstandings I've been talking about. It's an illusion. The illusion of judgment. Followed by the illusion of condemnation. It has been written: Judge not, and neither condemn.[8]

Interesting, isn't it, how quickly the very people who wish to reject the heart of Jesus' message are always first to quote Him (or rather misquote Him)? They quote "judge not lest you be judged" as a tool to persuade us to keep silent on the moral ills of our day. Or "love your neighbor as yourself," which of course they have satisfied because they lend their neighbor a lawn mower on occasion. Or they remind you that Jesus hobnobbed with tax collectors and sinners—as if His presence with them was for the purpose of condoning their sinful behavior. By taking His words or actions out of context, it's easy to make it seem as if Jesus were just this freewheelin' kind of guy who wouldn't think twice about someone doin' their own thing.

However, Matthew 7:1-5 states that we are not to judge hypocritically—not that we should always avoid making moral judgments. If I tell you it is wrong to steal while I am pilfering at Nordstrom, that would be a clear indication that I had better get the log out of my eye before I chastise you over the speck of dust in yours. Also, Walsch's young questioner had a right to be astonished at the idea that impending judgment by a holy God is illusory. I believe that at the very core of our being we intuitively know that Revelation 19:11 is an impending reality: "I saw heaven opened, and behold, a white horse, and He who sat on it is called Faithful and True, and in righteousness He judges and wages war."

Concerning "love your neighbor as yourself," those who quote it always seem to neglect the first and more important part of Jesus' words. In Matthew 22:36 a lawyer asked Jesus which commandment of the Law was the greatest. Jesus' response is found in verses 37-40.

> *He said to him, "'You shall love the Lord your God with all your heart, and with all your soul, and with all your mind.' This is the great and foremost commandment. The second is like it, 'You shall love your neighbor as yourself.' On these two commandments depend the whole Law and the Prophets."*

According to Jesus, we cannot have the second absent the first. We are to love God with all our heart, soul, and mind, first and foremost—which then gives us the ability to love our neighbor as ourself.

Additionally, as far as Jesus' fraternizing with those of questionable character, He certainly wasn't condoning their sinful behavior. In fact, He commented that the reason why He was with them was because they were spiritually and morally sick and needed a physician. He recognized that it was necessary to sit among them in order to bring them truth and freedom from their spiritual and moral illnesses because He, Jesus, has always been and still is in the business of radical life change.

Set Free by Jesus, the Truth

All the above is to say that the subjective view people hold of Jesus is a bit off the mark. Jesus, who is God (which qualifies Him as the One with the correct answers on spiritual and moral matters), believed in the reality of objective truth. After all, that's who He was and is. Jesus Christ is Truth. When we deny truth, we deny Jesus Christ. Consider the following passages about the reality and importance of truth:

- *John 1:17.* "The Law was given through Moses; grace and truth were realized through Jesus Christ."

- *John 8:31-32.* "So Jesus was saying to those Jews who had believed Him, 'If you continue in My word, then you are truly disciples of Mine; and you will know the truth, and the truth will make you free.'"

- *John 14:6.* "Jesus said to him, 'I am the way, and the truth, and the life; no one comes to the Father but through Me.'"

- *John 15:26.* "When the Helper comes, whom I will send to you from the Father, that is the Spirit of truth who proceeds from the Father, He will testify about Me."

- *John 17:17. Jesus, in His high-priestly prayer to the Father said,* "Sanctify them in truth; Your word is truth."

Truth matters. It sets us free, it sets us apart, it is not vague or illusive, and according to Jesus in the above passages, we can and will know it. The reality of the Christian faith is not "your truth" or "my truth." Praise God that by His beckoning it is truth that we *came to,* not that we invented.

And, morality is not a collection of ideas we create and change according to tradition or our whim at the moment. Moral absolutes are the same yesterday, today, and forever because they are rooted and grounded in the Truth—the very nature and character of the God who said, "I, the LORD, do not change."[9] How wonderful it is to be set free by truth, brought out of the bondage of deception to freedom in the Lord Jesus Christ.

Final Thoughts

Doesn't it seem crazy that we actually have to prove the existence of truth? There was a time when this wasn't the case. I think, though, that times can change yet again. I think the time just might be on the horizon for us to penetrate an invisible wall and reach those who have abandoned truth. Perhaps God will use you. I know He would like to. Since this is the case, I want to take a moment and offer some tools that may be helpful.

It is very important to open the lines of communication. When someone tells you that your truth is true for you only, it really can shut the whole conversation down...unless you ask one simple question. When chatting with someone who claims that truth is subjective, that there are no moral absolutes, or that all types of spiritual expression are equally valid, simply ask, "How do you know?" One of two things will happen.

One: Your acquaintance will attempt to defend her claim. The minute she begins an attempt to prove her position, you can lovingly point out her inconsistency in claiming there is no truth while claiming that her claim about truth is true. By doing this, you might just help her realize the bankruptcy of her position—and thus open the door for you to lovingly and enthusiastically share the good news.

Or two: Your acquaintance will not attempt to defend her claim because, if she is intellectually honest with you and herself, she will realize she has no idea why she believes what she believes.

If you notice irritation in her tone, it could simply be a result of a misunderstanding regarding what you believe. She assumes everyone holds the view that you can select any brand of religious expression because, to her, this is a matter of taste or opinion. Therefore, in essence she thinks that what you're saying is, "You will be separated from God forever if you don't like my brand of salad dressing."

The way to defuse the irritation is to point out a few things that I mentioned earlier. For instance, that this is not truth you invented but came to. You can also start with what is intuitive, what we all know is true, which was also covered in this chapter. The most important thing is to be patient. This worldview did not come about overnight. It's what many people, for years, have been conditioned to believe. Since it is so prevalent and, on the surface, sounds so appealing, it's going to take prayer and truth to breach the strongholds. Just like God is patient with you and me, let's try our best to be patient with our seeking family and friends. "The Lord is not slow about His promise, as some count slowness, but is patient toward you, not wishing for any to perish but for all to come to repentance."[10]

Questions for Reflection

1. *What is the difference between subjective and objective truth?*

2. *How would you respond to someone who makes the statement "Well, that's true for you" after you have just shared the gospel?*

3. *What are some differences between other world religions and Christianity?*

4. *Why do you believe that objective truth and moral absolutes matter? Is your answer just your personal opinion? How do you know?*

5. *Have you ever tried Cheez Doodles with peanut butter on them?*

Suggested Resources

Relativism: Feet Firmly Planted in Mid-Air by Francis J. Beckwith and Gregory Koukl. Baker Books, 1998.

The Death of Truth, general editor, Dennis McCallum. Bethany House Publishers, 1996.

The Universe Next Door: A Basic World View Catalog, third edition by James Sire. InterVarsity Press, 1997.

CHAPTER 5

Knowing Why Belief in Evolution Requires Enormous Faith

🐂

*T*he reason why humans no longer have fur is because they started wearing clothes."

"If Jesus had come at an earlier time during our evolutionary change He probably would have come as a monkey."

The subject of evolution sure tends to lend itself to some rather interesting speculations. The above statements, for instance, were serious thoughts offered by two highly successful professional women during a conversation we had about their position that evolution is a fact and creation is a religion. This is a popular position, to be sure. However, popularity really shouldn't be the basis by which we gauge the accuracy of a position.

I must confess that, for many years, I thought evolution made some sense. I mean, hey, the guy in the white lab coat with his reading glasses perched precariously upon the tip of his nose said it was so. Who was I to disagree with a learned scientist? Yet my nagging question remained: *Why are there still monkeys?*

But for me, things quickly changed. Once I gave my life to the Lord Jesus Christ, I simply adjusted the mechanism of evolution in my mind. Thus, I believed God used it to bring about the existence of human beings—mystery solved. My reason for holding that position,

I now admit, was a rather poor one. I believed that to hold to a literal creation account—God created everything in six days and it was all very good—and to believe in a worldwide flesh-flushing flood was a bit too anti-intellectual for a sharp gal like me. (Some brat, huh?)

It wasn't long before I realized that if I was going to believe the Bible as the truly inspired Word of God, I would have to take another look at the Genesis accounts of both creation and the flood. I saw that what I needed to do was to stop blaming God for a weak theory and consider the evidence, if any, that would substantiate the biblical accounts. It was worth the investigation, and I am delighted to have an opportunity to share with you what has become one of my favorite subjects. (I guess it's one of my favorites because the theory of evolution is great fodder for someone who enjoys taking the "reductio ad absurdum"—reducing to the absurd—approach when challenging others' thinking.)

With that in mind, I'd like to give a short review of the theory of evolution, and the implications of the theory. Then we'll look briefly at the fossil record to see if we can find any validity to the evolutionary claim. Afterward, we'll consider the biblical accounts of creation and the flood, since there is a connection between the flood and the fossils. What I think just might happen is that, by the end of this chapter, you'll see the theory of evolution not as science, but as an atheistic worldview that indeed requires enormous faith to believe.

In the Beginning, Nothing...
Then It Exploded

Perhaps you were taught, as I was during my years in grade school, the same particularly fantastic story about humankind's humble and rather insignificant emergence. The story went something like this: In the beginning (or, "once upon an eon") there was nothing—and by chance, it exploded. This explosion caused dust, gas, and radiation to whirl everywhere. Sprinkled with a little gravity, planets and stars formed from the particles of the original explosion, or big bang. For millions of years on our humble abode (earth), lightning flashed through an atmosphere of methane and ammonia. Then suddenly, for no reason and quite by chance, a group of molecules came together in primordial broth, reproduced, and life began. By chance, these new organisms grew and mutated. Because of their strong survival instinct, which they got just by chance, the stronger survived over the weaker. Through chance mutations and the death of weaker, less fortunate species, all creatures evolved into what we see today, including you and me. So to sum up, an explosion—disorder, that is—and chance occurrences brought forth order, intricate design, and *Homo sapiens.*

From Theory to Assumed Fact

Since the above does seem like a pretty good story, you would imagine that there must be some concrete evidence to support it. Especially because—and I'm not quite sure when it happened— somehow the theory of evolution seems to have become an assumed and accepted fact. Consider the matter-of-fact tone of a *Time* magazine article entitled "How Man Began."[1] In ever-so-small writing, underneath a rendering of our supposed above-average ancient forefather, who is running through the forest wearing nothing but a worried expression on his face, is this little tidbit of information concerning this *Homo erectus:*

> Accomplished ancestor: *Homo erectus* might not look like much, but he was the first creature to use fire, fashion advanced tools and leave mankind's African home.

Apparently the guy was brilliant. Perhaps the picture is of one *Homo erectus* in particular, the creature better known as Java man. They might have called him that because he was discovered on the island of Java, but I'd like to think that he simply enjoyed hanging out at the local Starbucks of his day. Maybe, since he was so advanced, they should have at least drawn him with a hot cup of joe in one hand and a briefcase in the other!

Fantastic stories regarding our supposed ancient ancestors don't end with the popular magazines or television shows of today. Simply take your children on a little outing. I'm sure you'll notice, if you haven't already, the evolutionary philosophy alluded to, or downright blatant, just about everywhere you go. It sure seems to me that the dogma is everywhere, from the aquarium to the zoo.

Even at my backyard volcano we could not escape indoctrination when we visited what has become known as the "blast zone." This dramatic landscape is located on the north side of Mount St. Helens. (Thankfully, our home is on the south side.) Just to give you a bit of background, during the nine-hour eruption on May 18, 1980, Mount St. Helens released the energy equivalent to a blast from 400 million tons of TNT. Now that's what I'd call a big bang. From the power of the blast, some areas were literally scraped down to the bedrock. Since what goes up must come down, debris and ash accumulated hundreds of feet thick on the landscape around the mountain. Ecologists in the area believed it would take a hundred years before life would return to the mountain, a landscape apparently totally devastated.

Yet to the amazement of all, especially the ecologists, it turned out that foliage actually seemed to grow well on the new landscape. Within two years of the eruption, 90 percent of all the original plant and wildlife had returned to Mount St. Helens.

At the visitors' center, after receiving this fascinating information on the return of plant and animal life, we were asked this question: "Do you know who the real hero is in the return of the plants and animals to Mount St. Helens?" Perhaps you and I just may be thinking of the same Person. Not, however, the guide at the visitors' center. Placing a gopher puppet on her hand, she proclaimed, "The gopher! You see, he burrowed into the ground before the eruption, and when it was over, on his way out he kicked up soil and seeds. Once the rains came, the seeds germinated, and other animals who eat those plants returned. Since the gopher couldn't find food, he eventually died, but his body became a meal for another animal. So even in death the gopher was the real hero."

Now, you may be wondering how this is an example of the theory of evolution. I share this experience because it demonstrates that glory is repeatedly given to the creature, not the Creator, which also seems to be an underlying theme of the theory.

The Rise of the Theory of Evolution

The theory of evolution is not a new worldview. It actually dates back to the ancient Greeks. However, its popularity really began to take off when Charles Darwin published his book *On the Origin of the*

Species in 1859 and later, in 1871, *The Descent of Man,* in which he posed the idea that human beings had evolved from lower life-forms. Darwin's writings offered what seemed like, to the minds of many, a sensible mechanism to explain away the Creator. Darwin thus paved the way for the scorning of Bible-believing Christians that followed. The most famous (or I should say, infamous) example would be what took place during the July 1925 Scopes "monkey trial."

What happened, in brief, was that the American Civil Liberties Union (ACLU) decided to solicit a teacher to challenge the Butler Act. This law forbade teachers to teach evolution in Tennessee public schools. In their quest to hunt up a willing candidate, they were able to persuade a physical-education teacher named John Scopes to become the defendant. Just so he could truthfully testify that he had in fact taught evolution, he instructed two students in the back of a taxi. (As it turned out, Scopes never took the witness stand—and after the trial, he wasn't really sure he ever had taught evolution.)

The famous criminal lawyer, and atheist, Clarence Darrow defended Scopes. Former presidential candidate, and Christian, William Jennings Bryan represented the state. By the fifth day of the trial a shift took place. The issue was no longer whether Scopes had violated the law, but whether creation or evolution was correct. Scopes was found guilty of violating the Butler Act and was fined $100, which Darrow promptly paid.

During the trial, however, reporters had flocked to Tennessee, and the media began to ridicule Christians for believing the Bible and the creation account. Because of the ridicule, Christians began to back away from the creation model. With the emergence of German higher theological criticism in the universities and churches across America, added to the decline of the nation's moral foundation, it became easy for evolution to rise to the popular platform we see it on today.

Unfortunately, what most people picture when they think of the Scopes "monkey trial" is the movie *Inherit the Wind,* a popular fictional account of the events in Tennessee during the summer of 1925. Less popular is the fact that many of the "proofs" of evolution used in the Scopes trial have now been flatly refuted through modern scientific study. And concerning the supposed "ape–men" that were cited as evidence, one turned out to be a hoax, one an ape, two fully human, and one—an extinct pig.

The Implications

"No single essential difference separates human beings from other animals." Quite a statement, wouldn't you say? That is the first line of the *Time* magazine article I mentioned earlier. In other words, there is no essential difference between a human being and a dog. Since the evolutionary position claims that humans are merely products of random chance, there was no pristine creation, no Creator to whom we are accountable, no fall from a state of innocence, and thus no need for the cross.

Think of it this way. If, for example, there is no intelligence behind the design, then there is no design—no meaning to what we behold. If everything from the stars in the heavenlies, to the lilies of the field, to you and me, is simply a product of random chance, then there is no Creator who has a plan and purpose for His creation or our lives. Once the Creator is dismissed, nothing restrains us from doing what is right in our own eyes, because neither is there a moral law. Now we can begin to tie in some of what I went over in the previous chapter.

With the dismissal of the moral law and Lawgiver, survival of the fittest dictates. Therefore, if you happen to be weak or sick, or you're in pain and are suffering, and if you are viewed simply as a financial burden to those around you, then it makes perfect sense to put you to sleep "compassionately"—like the old, unwanted house pet that has overstayed its welcome.

The implications are staggering, frightening, and as plain as the morning newspaper as to what a purposeless, random-chance worldview produces. The good news is that our belief in a Creator God is not just based upon the frightening logical implications of not believing in Him. We believe, as His Word states, because of the "convincing proofs," one of which is His handiwork that we behold "day to day...and night to night."

Let's Look at the Record

Every now and again, late, during those warmer-than-usual summer nights, I enjoy lounging around on my back deck to stargaze. The best time is during the new moon. It is pitch black out there at night in the forest, with no sign of city lights. I don't know if you've ever noticed it, but the longer you stare at the sky, the more stars you can see. Oh, I know, I know—it's just my eyes adjusting to the light (or lack of light, I should say), but it is still magnificent to behold. I have to tell you that it simply amazes me how anyone can gaze upon the heavenly bodies and remain thoroughly convinced that the existence of those bodies, as well as theirs, is simply the result of random-chance occurrences.

Chance...if you read the little plaques at your local zoo and listen to the evolutionary dogma long enough you'll realize there is no end to what *chance* can do. Thus, for the average evolutionist, this thing called *chance* is the perfect replacement for God, a fantastic story to explain away a personal Creator. After all, *chance* is powerful, *chance* has creative ability, and *chance* even improves upon what it creates! Unfortunately for those who cling tenaciously to this (which requires greater faith than belief in a personal Creator), as any mathematician can prove, *chance* can never be spelled with a capital *c*. The reason is simple—*chance* is nothing but a mathematical probability.

Though I regretfully confess that I truly did waste much of my time in grade school utilizing my desk as a headrest (that dear science teacher was more accurate than she knew), I do recall the mantra, "What chance creates, chance destroys."

Imagine for a moment that my husband, Jeff, and I are going to play a game of Scrabble. Imagine that Jeff places a handful of tiles in the cup, shakes them vigorously, spills them onto the board—and by random chance the tiles fall in such a way that they spell the words JEFF LOVES JUDY. Would those words, in that case, have any meaning or purpose? The answer is no. Why? Because after Jeff and I have a good laugh about it, as quickly as he can scoop up those letters and spill them out again order will become disorder, or..."*what chance creates, chance destroys*" and the letters will probably read something like JLU FEDJ YVFE OS.

Now, imagine that instead of simply spilling the tiles onto the playing board, Jeff handpicks the tiles one by one from the cup as I sit there, probably batting my eyes at him. If he carefully spells out the words JEFF LOVES JUDY, suddenly those letters have meaning and purpose. The meaning is that he loves me, and the purpose is his desire to communicate that message to me. The difference between the first scenario and the second is that there is intelligence behind the design. (Exactly like the *God* billboard I spoke of in chapter 2.)

Again, what chance creates, chance destroys. This basic principle is completely contrary to the theory of evolution. Evolution proposes that we should see advancement, or betterment, of creatures through chance mutations as time goes on. Yet in reality we don't see that at all. What we do witness is an increase of disease and death, and in many cases, extinction.

Mutation Is Malformation

That something mutates is not a sign that evolution is a fact. Mutation is like decay—a dead carcass has to exist for the decay to set in. A creature had to exist at one time in a pure, perfect state in order for it to mutate. Therefore the question remains: How did the creature get here in the first place? To throw in the idea of mutation doesn't answer the question—it only creates a new one. Again, since nothing mutates for the better, random-chance mutations certainly don't help a critter—they hinder.

Perhaps you never forget a face either. For me, names yes, faces no. I will especially never forget one face in particular. I saw it when I was just 18 years old as I was walking through the halls of Cornell University in Ithaca, New York. There it was, floating in a jar of formaldehyde—the head of a lamb with cyclopian malformation. With only one eye in the center, it was a miniature Cyclops! Just in case you are curious, here is how this condition occurs. If by chance a pregnant ewe, on her fourteenth day of gestation, eats the herb *Veratrum californicum*, toxic alkaloids in the plant cause the cyclopian malformation—or, as the condition is more affectionately known, monkey face.[2] Trust me—it doesn't look anything like a monkey. Now, are we to believe that random-chance processes are a good and help-ful thing to the creature? Are we to assume that, given enough time, the little Cyclops will adjust to its malformation and thus improve and survive?

Let us, for a moment, grant the evolutionist the premise of random-chance mutations as a mechanism for the arrival of all the creatures we see today. Perhaps the lungfish, a fascinating creature I met at the zoo, could help explain just how he arrived at his special survival mechanism. Here is a fish that lives in drought-prone areas. When riverbeds completely dry up, the fish will burrow into the bottom mud and form a mucusy cocoon around itself. Because it actually possesses lungs, it can breathe, and thus it can survive in its cocoon for quite some time. When the rains return, the river fills up, and the lungfish emerges from its long siesta. Now, granting the evolutionary premise, did the lungfish call a meeting and say to its fishy friends and family, "You know, I've been thinking, every year when the drought comes we all die. Next year, why don't we develop some lungs, then create little cocoons and curl up in them for a few months until the rains return? What do you say we give it a whirl and see how it goes?" That's pretty silly, huh? Obviously, unless on the very first go-round they had figured it out, they would all be dead.

I can only imagine just how many other organs in the lungfish would have had to "mutate" right along with its intentionally evolved, perfectly working lungs. Right along with its new lungs would also have to be the development of the necessary apparatus to give it the ability to construct its mucusy cocoon. (By the way, if the creature has the ability to figure it out, what room is there for random chance?

Obvious Monkey Business

In spite of the mounting evidence against the evolutionary hypothesis, the proponents of this worldview seem to become more creative every day. A few years ago I read a rather humorous little item in my local newspaper about what some hail as a possible link from beast to man. The article was entitled "Tall and Meaty, Bigfoot Lumbers Around."[3] Included was a drawing of a large, powerful-looking, furry creature. Point by point, the creature was meticulously described: its eating habits, demeanor, height, weight, strength, movement, eyesight, hearing, sense of smell, noises it made, and of course its foot size. The punchline summed up the whole matter quite nicely, including a factoid that began, "Generally accepted scientific evidence of the species." It was completed with one word. Can you guess what that one word was that described the "generally accepted scientific evidence"? Here it is…"none." (Why was this *news?*)

The best part of the entire item was noted off to the side with an icon of a telephone above it. It read, "Bigfoot Unplugged—what does a Bigfoot sound like? To listen to some strange sounds that researchers claim may be Bigfoot caught on tape, call the Info-line." I called the number supplied, and all I heard was banjo music. Apparently, Bigfoot was either truly "unplugged"...or had evolved with hidden talents that even the learned scientists had neglected to mention.

Since my humorous Bigfoot article is a few years old, I decided to get an update on the latest in the ape–men–monkey mystery. So I e-mailed Professor Frank Sherwin, zoologist with the Institute for Creation Research and international creation-science lecturer and debater, to get the latest scoop on *who is hot* and *who is not*. The following was his summation:

> The case for "human evolution" continues to be mired in controversy. The secular community states the best link between man and his alleged apelike ancestor is *Australopithecus*—which means *southern ape*. Creation scientists maintain that's exactly what the shattered fossil remains show—an extinct ape. Everything about this creature was apelike. Even evolutionist Meg Rudolph called *Australopithecus* a "hodge-podge genus" (*Geotimes,* May 2001)! Daniel Lieberman is an expert on "human evolution" and admitted in *Nature* magazine (March 2001) that "the evolutionary history of humans is complex and unresolved." Henry Gee, again in *Nature* (one of the most well established science publications in the world) said, "Fossil evidence of human evolutionary history is fragmentary and open to various interpretations" (July 2001).
>
> Is this why "human evolution" should be taught as fact in taxpayer-funded public schools? Since our public educational domain is supposedly the free marketplace of ideas, would it not be refreshing to have quotes like the above free and open to American public school children?

As a mom, I think he makes a pretty good point.

The Missing "Missing Link"

Now, I hate to throw another Bogart classic film at you, but have you ever watched *The Cain Mutiny?* Humphrey Bogart played a shell-shocked, overworked, hard-driving, paranoid World War II ship captain. During a voyage, a gallon of strawberries mysteriously vanished.

Even though he was informed that a couple of sailors had confessed to eating the strawberries, the captain was determined to find a missing duplicate key which he, using "geometric logic," theorized someone had created and used to break into a cabinet containing the coveted strawberries. His thinking was, find the duplicate key and he would find the strawberry thief. The captain was so certain his theory was correct that in the middle of the night he had the entire ship turned upside down to find a key, though deep down inside he knew that it existed only in his mind. Bizarre behavior, to be sure.

Yet, like the ship captain in *The Cain Mutiny*, who was looking for the missing duplicate key to substantiate his theory, so too is the evolutionist looking for the missing link to substantiate his. The truth is, the missing link, like the key, is simply not missing—because it doesn't exist. However, to call it "missing" assumes its existence. They use the term "missing" because it seems pretty silly to search for something that you only imagine exists—or that you know, deep down inside, couldn't possibly exist. The evolutionist approaches his subject with a huge presupposition: that there is a missing link, Big Foot or small, to substantiate his theory.

Of course, the creationist also approaches the subject of origins with a presupposition: that there is a Creator God. The difference is, when you sincerely search for the Creator you find Him because, as the apostle Paul stated in Acts 17, "He is not far from each one of us," in addition to the fact that He actually does exist!

Of the millions of fossils in museums around the globe, there is not one showing that any animal has ever evolved into another. There simply are no transitional forms. Neither has any "missing link" between man and any other animal ever been found. Every skull, jaw, tooth, and bone fragment has proved to be either a hoax, fully human, or fully animal. The following is a list of what some of the most popular finds have turned out to be:

- Java man: an ape

- "Lucy": a chimpanzee

- Neanderthal: fully human

- Nebraska man: a wild pig

- Peking man: no physical evidence for its existence

- Piltdown man: a human skull and an ape's jaw

- Ramapithicus: an orangutan

- "Toumai" (found in the spring of 2002): most likely a gorilla or chimp

Chickens? Or Created?

In another imaginative attempt to support the evolutionary hypothesis, some scientists proposed what they called the "protein clock" theory. This theory was supposed to "pin down with great precision" when humans branched off into mammals. Unfortunately for the evolutionists, after the theory was tested, it turned out that humans were more closely related to chickens than they were to mammals, including the apes. Can you just imagine the names they would have assigned to our supposed ancient ancestors? *Australopithecus* would be *Australochickenus* or *Bock-Bockosithicus*, or maybe *Paleobird-brainenus*, or perhaps even *Neanderclaws!* If it weren't so sad, it would be funny.

Once again, Professor Frank Sherwin lends his insights:

> Investigating the record of rocks (the fossils) for physical validation of the Darwinian process has revealed…nothing. One of the ironies of Darwin's infamous book, *On the Origin of the Species,* is that he never addressed the origin of species! In the 21st Century the secular community is still investigating the origin of species. Ironically, Dr. A.G. Fisher in the 2002 edition of the prestigious *Grolier Multimedia Encyclopedia* stated, "Both the origin of life and the origin of the major groups of animals remains unknown." Unknown, ever since Darwin—but they're still looking. Meanwhile, the Christian has a Book that very clearly describes the origin (and destiny!) of the species.

Amen to that. Admissions of the weakness of the theory abound, and not just in *Grolier's Multimedia Encyclopedia.* The tide is shifting, and some researchers, realizing the bankruptcy of the evolutionary hypothesis, are bold enough to admit it. Consider what Sir Fred Hoyle and Chandra Wickramasinghe once wrote:[4]

The likelihood of the spontaneous formation of life from inanimate matter is one to a number with 40,000 noughts [zeroes] after it...It is big enough to bury Darwin and the whole theory of evolution. There was no primeval soup, neither on this planet or any other, and if the beginnings of life were not random, they must therefore have been the product of purposeful intelligence.

Somehow, I am reminded of 1 Corinthians 1:20. "Where is the wise man? Where is the scribe? Where is the debater of this age? Has not God made foolish the wisdom of the world?"

A Turn to the Word

Evolution certainly does seem to require quite a bit of faith. However, since we place our faith in a Divine Creator, we'll turn to the Scriptures to look at further reasons for such faith. Taking your time to absorb the text, read Genesis 1:1–2:3. As you read, you just might want to underline the phrase "and there was evening and there was morning," and circle every occurrence of the phrases "after their kind" and "after its kind."

The Days

The text shows by modifying "day" with "evening" and "morning" that each day could certainly have been a 24-hour period. There seems to be no ambiguity in the text regarding the length of each day. Not only is each "day" modified with "evening" and "morning," but the text also includes the number of each day. There is no reason to imagine that these were indeterminate periods of time, longer or shorter than 24 hours. I point this out because, as I stated earlier, I used to believe that God used evolution as the mechanism for the creative process. Therefore, each day had to, I thought, represent long periods of time. But the text refuted me flatly.

I think what could be more of a puzzle is why God would take as long as six days to create. Why would it take a God who can create *ex nihilo* (out of nothing) six days to accomplish the task? Surely He could have done the whole thing in an instant. Perhaps He, being our perfect and supreme Parent, was setting an example for His children. God commanded us to work six days and rest on the seventh.

Remember the sabbath day, to keep it holy...For in six days the LORD *made the heavens and the earth, the sea and all that is in them, and rested on the seventh day; therefore the* LORD *blessed the sabbath day and made it holy.*[5]

On the seventh day, God rested from His work. Now, I would have to agree with others who suggest that God, who does not need to rest, was simply alluding to the end of the process of creation. After the sixth day, it seems that no new life forms were created. That is certainly consistent with what we see in nature. No new life forms are emerging—rather, many have died away or are dying away.

The Kinds

All right, count 'em up—did you arrive at ten? Did you notice that the phrases "after their kind" or "after its kind" appear ten times in the first chapter of the book of Genesis with regard to how living things reproduce? Yet again, God is right on target scientifically, this time about gene structure. Indeed, all living things reproduce "after their kind." Living things, over the years, do not mutate into completely different species. They can't, because DNA makes that impossible. What a shame it is that Charles Darwin, who was not a scientist but earned a degree in theology from Cambridge University, knew nothing about DNA, which carries the genetic codes. This is rather important, because a genetic code is preprogrammed into every living thing. Had Darwin known about the genetic code, perhaps he would have abandoned his theory before publication, since the codes are what make evolution, as Darwin suggested it, impossible.

I guess the best way to explain the genetic code is by a simple illustration. Just suppose, as I was sitting at my computer typing away, I boasted, "My computer is so smart that whenever I misspell a word, it figures out what I've done wrong—and to save me from embarrassment, it corrects the mistakes all on its own!" Would that statement be accurate? What if I decided to leave my computer on for eons with the Microsoft Word program open, in hope that it would someday evolve into the Mavis Beacon Teaches Typing program? Would that be a good idea? Would Word eventually become Mavis, or would I simply be left with an enormous electric bill?

My boasts about my computer being smart would not be accurate, and neither would it be a good idea to run up my electric bill. The reason is this: My computer isn't smart—the intelligent computer programmer is. It took an intelligence independent of the computer system to create the initial program to make it do what it does. For this same reason, no matter how much time is added to the equation, Word will never evolve into Mavis.

Just as my computer did not create its own computer programs, likewise, plants, parasites, pets, and people did not create their own genetic codes. Each genetic code was preprogrammed by our intelligent Creator, who is independent of the system. This is why lungfish can survive underneath riverbeds and why monkeys cannot turn into men.

Even the Creation Groans

God called His creation "very good." Random chance and mutations do not result in what one would consider "very good." All you have to do is consider cyclopian malformation to know that's true. By Genesis 3, the entire creation was suffering because of the sin of Adam and Eve. When I think of that poor creature, that little lamb born with no hope for survival, I think of Romans 8:20-22:

> *The* creation was subjected to futility, *not willingly, but because of Him who subjected it, in hope that the creation itself also will be set free from its slavery to corruption into the freedom of the glory of the children of God. For we know that the* whole creation groans and suffers *the pains of childbirth together until now.*

Water, Water, Everywhere—
That's How Fossils Form

I have always wondered how long it was between the creation and the fall. The Scriptures seem to be silent with regard to that. However, we do know that after the fall, humanity deteriorated rather quickly in its morality. Within just the first generation, the first murder was committed. After a time, the world became so corrupt that "every intent of the thoughts of his [mankind's] heart was only evil continually."[6] What a horrible place. As recorded in Genesis 6, God was "grieved in His heart" and proposed to judge the earth by water.

Thankfully, though it must have seemed a crazy thing to do at the time, faithful Noah responded to God's command to build an ark, along with his three sons. The ark, or barge, was one of enormous capacity at 450 feet long, 75 feet wide, and 45 feet high—certainly large enough to house the animals the Lord would draw into it. As it turned out, the barge would be a vessel of salvation for just eight persons and a myriad of animals. "Essence of Ark"—it must have been quite odiferous, yet better to be inside than outside, to be sure.

Since many people picture the flood account as depicted in cartoon drawings, as simply an easy-does-it boat ride with the animals smiling away at Noah, let's look at the actual account:

> The flood came upon the earth for forty days, and the water increased and lifted up the ark, so that it rose above the earth. The water prevailed and increased greatly upon the earth, and the ark floated on the surface of the water. The water prevailed more and more upon the earth, so that all the high mountains everywhere under the heavens were covered. The water prevailed fifteen cubits [22½ feet] higher, and the mountains were covered. All flesh that moved on the earth perished, birds and cattle and beasts and every swarming thing that swarms upon the earth, and all mankind; of all that was on the dry land, all in whose nostrils was the breath of the spirit of life, died. Thus He blotted out every living thing that was upon the face of the land, from man to animals to creeping things and to birds of the sky, and they were blotted out from the earth; only Noah was left, together with those that were with him in the ark. The water prevailed upon the earth one hundred and fifty days.[7]

A pretty dramatic picture, wouldn't you say? In Genesis 7:11 the text states that "all the fountains of the great deep burst open, and the floodgates of the sky were opened." Therefore, it wasn't just a nice, light, steady rain, as some might think. There was dramatic tectonic activity in the earth that made "all," not just some, but "all the fountains of the great deep" to burst open. Incredible.

The Evidence Today Is Consistent with Genesis

When I read the account, I must admit that I find it difficult to accept, as some people have suggested, that the flood of Noah was simply a local event. That thinking seems to be refuted by logic, the geological evidence, and the text itself. After all, how could the water cover the highest local mountain without running downhill into another region? (Is it possible that someone else could have erected a wall around the locale of the flood higher than the highest mountain?)

Further, if the flood had been a local event, you would think that God could have done something simpler than have Noah construct a massive vessel. After all, God simply sent angels to lead Lot and his family away from one local event—the destruction of the city of Sodom. Surely, within a period of 120 years, He could have brought Noah and his family quite a distance away from a "local" flood. Why bother with building an ark? Why bother bringing a vast array of animals to that ark, rather than just leading them out of the region of Mesopotamia?

However, there's exciting evidence for a worldwide flood all around us. Globally, there are mass graves of fully formed fossils in muddy sediments that were rapidly laid down by water. This is exactly how fossils form, by things being buried swiftly or catastrophically— they cannot form over millions of years because decay would erode any trace of them. Since there are no "transitional" forms in these sediments, some evolutionists use the term "abrupt appearance" to explain away the existence of fully formed creatures, catastrophically preserved for all to see.

It amazes me just how incredibly powerful water is and what sort of damage it can inflict in an extremely short amount of time. If you visit the north side of Mount St. Helens, you will observe a small-scale "Grand Canyon," not formed over millions of years by the gentle movement of Spirit Lake as it was before the eruption, but catastrophically in a matter of hours.

Another fascinating piece of evidence for a global flood is that the traditions of about 270 people groups around the world tell of a time when the entire world was destroyed by flood, both man and beast. They also tell of a vessel of safety provided for a small group of survivors. This is exactly what you would expect from cultures around the world who had formerly been one happy family around Babel, but were then dispersed throughout the world. Unfortunately, without good Jewish scribes in their camps, the stories were not preserved accurately through time and thus have variations. Yet the core of the account remains the same.

There also exists rather interesting eyewitness testimony of a huge vessel on the mountains of Ararat. Though individuals have offered their testimony at differing times and without contact with each other, their accounts seem to be perfectly consistent. They all seem to report seeing a vessel in the biblical location, partly covered, partly exposed—with a stair-step topography leading up to it.

What we observe today is consistent with what we should observe if the biblical accounts are true. And I haven't even touched upon concerns about the accuracy of current dating methods used on rocks and fossils. However, I think enough evidence has been presented to show you that God's Word, once again, is right on.

God indeed judged the world with water, and by His love and mercy He then set a bow in the sky as a promise that He would never again judge the world by a flood. However, as the sin of Cain intensifies, and evil and debauchery increase, we must remember that He also promised He would judge the world again before He completely restores it, but the next time, by fire.

Final Thoughts

When I think of what God has done with my life in the time since I submitted it to Him, it amazes me. You would never recognize Judy B.C. with Judy A.D. I certainly praise and thank Him for that—it's just another piece of evidence that God can make something of nothing.

I will give thanks to the LORD with all my heart;
I will tell of all Your wonders.
I will be glad and exult in You;
I will sing praise to Your name, O Most High.[8]

Therefore,

Serve the LORD with gladness;
Come before Him with joyful singing.

> *Know that the* LORD *Himself is God; it is He who has made*
> *us, and not we ourselves.*
> *We are His people and the sheep of His pasture.*[9]

Yes, He is the One who has made us and "not we ourselves." This is one reason why I think God created us last. Perhaps God wanted to prove to humankind that He didn't need our help, advice, or ingenuity during the creation process. If we could, surely we would somehow attempt to take credit for what "God hath wrought." I think we all know unbelieving individuals who boldly proclaim, "If it were me, I would have created it this way." Wouldn't it be fun, at just such a moment, to hear the Lord of all creation thunderously respond from the heavenlies,

> *Now gird up your loins like a man,*
> *And I will ask you, and you instruct Me!*
> *Where were you when I laid the foundation of the earth?*
> *Tell Me, if you have understanding.*[10]

With Job, I can imagine their response in chorus: "Behold, I am insignificant; what can I reply to You? I lay my hand on my mouth."[11] Sometimes, isn't that just an awfully good place for it?

Questions for Reflection

1. *Can you name three reasons why evolution requires enormous faith?*

2. *What is it about every living thing that negates the possibility of one species evolving into another?*

3. *What phrase in the Word of God tells us just how all living things reproduce?*

4. *What are some of the implications of believing we are simply products of random chance?*

5. *Have you ever seen the movie* Inherit the Wind?

Suggested Resources

Creation Scientists Answer Their Critics by Duane T. Gish, Ph.D. Institute for Creation Research, 1993. I highly recommend you contact ICR at <www.icr.org/store> for a full line of wonderful materials related to this subject.

The Illustrated Origins Answers Book: Concise, Easy-to-Understand Facts About the Origin of Life, Man, and the Cosmos, third edition, by Paul S. Taylor. Films for Christ Assn., 1995.

The Long War Against God: The History and Impact of the Creation/Evolution Conflict by Dr. Henry Morris. Master Books, 2000.

CHAPTER 6

Reasons for the Existence of Evil and Suffering

ook, Mommy, isn't she so pretty? She's an angel! I want to hold her, Mommy!" I stopped loading my groceries onto the conveyer belt at the checkout stand to see what had so charmed my then three-year-old daughter Nicole's tender heart. She pointed excitedly as my eyes fixed upon the "angel" in question. Dressed in an exquisite costume with soft, fluffy, white feathers surrounding her beautiful form, it was none other than JonBenet Ramsey, pictured on the cover of a tabloid magazine.

Encircling the photo of this precious and lovely little girl were words describing her brutal death. The contrast of utter innocence (Nicole's sweet response and that darling child's picture) and utter evil (the murder of that beautiful little girl) took my breath away. I was thankful that Nicole had not mastered reading yet, as it would have broken her heart to have known the truth.

"Sweetheart, she really is an angel, isn't she?" was my sorrowful response. After that experience I just kept wondering how I would ever explain to her just how evil the human heart can be. (Yet only God knows its depths.)

We hear it on the news, we read it in the newspapers, we see it in our lives and in the lives of family and friends around us...and the questions abound. Since September 11, I'm sure I'm not the only one

115

who has received countless telephone and e-mail messages questioning God's role and the existence of evil. So let's answer them.

While there are several facets to what is considered "evil," I think the most common concerns are human suffering, and the evil acts committed by humans upon humans. With that in mind, first we'll consider the problem of evil in the world from our perspective. Then we will take a look at who's really to blame for its existence. Afterward, I will show you that, though we don't have all the answers, God does indeed work all things together for good—it's just that His definition and ours might be a bit different, as you'll soon see. Finally, since I think it is important to address the subject on a fiercely practical level, I will discuss ways in which you can minister to individuals who may face a crisis of belief because of a particular facet of this issue in their own lives.

Our Myopic Perspective

Whenever this topic arises, I can't help but remember a brief conversation I once had with an older gentleman who dismissed God completely because of the existence of evil and human suffering. His anger toward God was obvious as he swore and then bitterly proclaimed, "There is no God." That gentleman's passion and mine prompted me to ask him how he had arrived at his conclusion. He replied, "Listen, I was in World War II, and I saw what went on in those concentration camps. And I can assure you, with the horror that went on there, there can be no God."

How telling his response was. That gentleman and others like him intuitively know something about the character of God. That if God exists, He would be good, and just, and loving—and possessing these attributes, He would certainly not allow evil to occur. The veteran's conclusion, I think, is a reasonable one. For many people like him, the following questions remain:

1. If God is all-good, and created everything very good, why is there evil in the world?

2. Why did God allow evil to creep into His very good creation, and why doesn't He wipe it out of existence?

3. If God created all things, did He also create evil?

4. How can perfect creatures of God produce evil?

Tough questions, to be sure, and they simply don't come with trite, easy answers. Though there are no easy answers, I think *an* answer can lie in first addressing some common perceptions or misconceptions.

An Upside-Down View

Often, when something horrible happens to someone "really nice," the reaction is, "They don't deserve something like that to happen to *them!*" Why? Because most people believe that if you are a *good person*, all of life should be a joy because *good* things happen to *good people*. On the flip side of that buffalo nickel, if you are a *not-so-nice person* and *bad* things happen to you, you simply deserved it.

Therefore, if life doesn't measure up to this basic rule of ours, we call it "injustice"—and begin to blame God. Immediately, we lose any eternal perspective we had, and the creature accuses the Creator. Yet, shall the pot say to the Potter, "What's up with that?"

When we do this, instead of leaning on His divine sovereignty we mistakenly stand as His accuser. The thinking, *How can such an awful thing happen to a nice person like me?* can perhaps come from a faulty notion that God created us simply to make us happy. Therefore, when pain enters our lives, or when we suffer a loss, we tend to question His goodness, His power, and finally, His very existence. We think, *How can this awful thing be the will of a good God who supposedly loves me?*

Perhaps the first questions we should ask are, *Why did God create us, if not to make us happy? What is our ultimate purpose?* I think the answer is best summed up in the old Westminster Shorter Catechism.[1] Question 1 reads, "What is the chief end of man?" Perhaps some would answer it this way: "Man's chief end is to glorify his things, and to enjoy himself forever." However, as you and I know, that certainly is not the answer. The answer to question 1 of the Catechism is, "Man's chief end is to glorify *God*, and to enjoy *Him* forever" (emphasis mine).

In light of that, there must be more to suffering than what our emotions tell us. Our emotions can sometimes make us believe that it is all for nothing. So, when we experience pain, or loss, or suffering, our temporal perspective immediately kicks in and we lose our eternal perspective. Again, the primary problem is in our perception—a perception that is skewed by our fallen nature and by our propensity to focus only on the here and now instead of the hereafter. It is skewed by the fact that our fallen nature distorts our view of God. Therefore, some individuals, instead of trusting in His sovereignty, accuse Him—as if evil were somehow His fault because He hasn't wiped it out.

Who, Me?

So here we are back at square one. If God is all-good and all-powerful He can and should wipe out all evil, and He is cruel and unjust for not annihilating all evil. It is certainly true that God could, at any moment, wipe out all evil. People know this intuitively. However, if God annihilated all evil, then *all* evil—both actual and potential—would be annihilated. Absent the cross, that would have to include you and me as well. He would have to wipe us out on the basis of the actual evil we've committed and our future or potential evil.

If perhaps you are thinking, as others do, that you would be exempt from such a broad-brush evil eradication, let me make a suggestion. How about if at your next ladies' "Mug and Muffin" fellowship time, everyone brings their favorite coffee mug and some fresh-baked pastries while you provide a video of the past 24 hours of your thought life? Now, close your eyes and think about what we'd all get to see. Do you think anyone would want to sit next to you the following Sunday? (Don't worry—my video wouldn't fare any better.)

My dear sister, not one of us is above the crimes we read about or the depravity we vigorously oppose. Heaven help us if we ever think we are. Jesus said that if you even look at someone with contempt in your heart, it is equivalent to murder, and therefore it must be dealt with before the throne of grace. We all violate God's holy character, both in thought and in deeds done or neglected.

Since the problem of evil actually directs us to the character of God, I have to ask these questions: What is more merciful? What is more loving? For God to annihilate those made in His image, who have abused their gift of free choice and still abuse that gift—or to have made a provision for it through the cross of Jesus Christ? Would it be better for Him to eradicate us—or to use sin, sickness, and suffering for a greater purpose? Which is of greater virtue? Certainly, the greater virtue is that He use our miserable temporary circumstances for His higher and eternal purposes. Again, if God were to wipe out all evil He would be the only One left. That act would defeat the very purpose for which He created us: true and honest, free-choice, non-robotic fellowship with Him, our Creator.

The good news is that God ultimately *will* defeat and overcome evil and restore His creation once again to "very good" status. What we're left with for now is the best possible world that can operate under the cloud of the fall. How thankful I am for His mercy in not annihilating all evil but working His will in spite of and in the face of it. By His grace, since He has not yet defeated evil, everyone has an opportunity to come to trust and believe in Him.

Does "All-Power" Mean Anything Goes?

But again the challenges abound: *If God is all-powerful and benevolent He would destroy all evil. If God doesn't destroy all evil, perhaps He is all-powerful and not benevolent, but malevolent—because how can a good God bear to see His creatures suffer from evil? Or, perhaps He is benevolent but not all-powerful—therefore He cannot destroy all evil. And if that is the case, that God is not all-powerful, perhaps there is no God at all.*

However, all this is a misunderstanding of what it means that God possesses omnipotence, or all-power. Omnipotence does not mean that God can do absolutely anything. There are things He cannot do. He cannot do anything that would violate His other attributes—this is why He cannot lie. And no, He cannot make a rock so big He can't move it, as some philosophers like to pose, because—as it's been well said—"God doesn't do dumb things." However, aside from that, He will not make something so big that He cannot control it. God cannot do anything that is actually impossible, and it is actually impossible to destroy evil without destroying free choice—and free choice is necessary to a moral universe.

Since God cannot do what is contrary to His nature, He cannot be blamed for that which He cannot do. He cannot give human beings free choice sometimes and not other times. He cannot create beings as free moral agents, then snap His fingers and make them robots whenever they stray from His will. God cannot create beings with free choice and then force them to make right choices. If that were the case, they would not be free moral agents who have the responsibility and capacity to choose to bless or curse Him.

Evil's Source

My mom is an artist. You name it, she's done it—in just about every medium. She is also extremely crafty, but in a good way. Walking through her house is a lot of fun because you will notice creative little things and ask, "Where did you get this?" To which her response usually is, "Oh, they wanted 30 bucks for it, so I decided to make it myself for a dollar." It's sort of a family joke. For years I kidded her, saying I was sure she made her huge oriental rugs as she rode to work on the number 13 bus. Not long ago she taught herself how to paint in watercolor—and then proceeded to win an award for what was to her simply an attempt at the medium.

Now, have you ever witnessed an artist at work? They place the smallest brushstroke on the canvas, then lean back in their chair to observe. Again and again: small stroke, lean back and observe... correct...change...add...observe.

When I think of Genesis 1:31, I picture an artist, only this Artist had to lean back and observe His creation only once. "God saw all that He had made, and behold, it was very good." In the beginning our Creator, the only appropriate One to judge creation, completed and then beheld His own handiwork. Just as an artist places one last stroke upon a canvas with her brush and then leans back to observe, so too, God beheld His creation and deemed it very good. Since the very core of God's nature is goodness, everything He does is "very good," including His creation, as described in Genesis 1 and 2.

Evil is *not* "very good." I know, I know—and as the younger generation would say in a singsong tone, "Duh!" But just hang in there with me. First, we must realize that God did not create this world the way we see it today. The Creator of our first parents bestowed upon them, as part of being image-bearers, the very good gift and power of free choice. With their free choice, our first parents chose evil, abusing their gift by rebelling against God.

What we now experience are the results of the abuse of a very good gift our perfect heavenly Parent bestowed upon those He created in His image—namely, the freedom and power to make choices for good or for evil. While in their state of innocence, Adam and Eve abused God's gift of free choice and chose to rebel against His sole restriction upon them.

Although God did make evil possible, individual human beings alone are responsible for actually carrying it out by the choices they make. It's just like what my mom-in-law says about her diet: "It's all about choices." That goes for carrot sticks or Oreo cookies, love or hate, good or evil, praising God or shaking our fist at Him. Nevertheless, the fact that humanity would choose evil was the risk God was willing to take to enjoy free-will fellowship with us.

We might wonder why God would even put that tempting tree of the knowledge of good and evil in the midst of the Garden. We might well reason, *If it weren't for that stinkin' tree, we wouldn't be in the mess we are in right now.* Yet without the tree, our first parents really wouldn't have had free choice. To illustrate this concept, say, for example, that I have asked you to come for a visit to my home, and I've told you that you can travel on any road you desired to reach me. With your free choice, you look at a map to select which road you wish to take…only to find that there is only one road leading over-the-river-and-through-the-woods.

Now, was it true that you could take any road you desired? No, it wasn't true. You did not have an opportunity to exercise your free choice since there was only one road reaching my home. It is the same with the tree. Without an opportunity to choose to obey and not eat, or to choose to disobey and eat, the creature does not have free choice or free will at all.

Didn't He Create…Everything?

Obviously God was not the creator of evil. What He created was a perfect universe without sin, without suffering, and without evil. Evil came into this world by a willful act of disobedience toward a loving heavenly Father, who knew the consequences for it would be great and warned our first parents of it.

Keep in mind that God created all substances. Evil, however, is not a thing or a substance. Evil is just like mutation (see chapter 5). The creature has to exist for the mutation to corrupt it. Therefore, evil is the corruption of God's very good creation that already existed.

Whine, Whine, Whine, Whine, Whine!

Some people may object and say, "Why do I have to suffer for the sins of the Adam's family?" Think of it this way. If perfectly innocent human beings living in a gloriously beautiful environment where they would never know want—beings who enjoyed such purity of fellowship with God and each other that in their nakedness they did not experience shame—would choose evil, how much more would we make that same choice in our current fallen condition? How wonderful it is to know that because God is good and just and loving, His remedy for sin and evil is for everyone. How wonderful it is that "choose you this day whom you will serve" is still a decision we can make by the exercise of our free will and by the drawing of the Holy Spirit.

Romans 8:28...Not Just Something to Quote!

At the intellectual level, and perhaps the spiritual, what I've shared just might suffice in addressing the problem of evil and human suffering. However, I think it is vitally important to address this subject on the fiercely practical level. After all, that is where we live. To do this I thought I would share with you the circumstances surrounding a little baby boy who made a huge impact on not only a tiny mountain community but on friends and family members across this country, and—who knows—from this writing, perhaps eventually the world.

I must tell you that, as far as births are concerned, I have never seen a baby more anticipated by an entire community than little Kenneth Hubbell, due May 20, 2001. The number of people at Carol Hubbell's shower was truly a blessing. It included many individuals, male and female, who I had never met before. It was great fun sitting in a large circle in our fellowship hall, passing gift after gift around the room that Carol had just excitedly received and unwrapped. The gifts included beautiful handmade bedding and clothes; baby toys, cartons of diapers and baby wipes; and everything else you could imagine that an expectant mom would need.

Kenneth was child number six, with the older siblings ranging from age 17 to age 10. For 42-year-old Carol, he was little Mr. Surprise, Surprise! With finances extremely tight, she was very grateful for her shower, viewing it as a blessing of a lifetime.

On May 11, I received an urgent phone call from our prayer-warrior chain. Carol was in the hospital. She hadn't felt the baby move that morning and became concerned. Fervent prayers rang out from throughout our little valley and from friends and family members across the country that, by God's grace, Kenneth and Carol would be okay.

I have, as I'm sure you have as well, fervently prayed for many expected little ones who faced some sort of unexpected complication. I will tell you, I have never had this experience before, but as I fervently prayed for this child's life, I strangely felt the Spirit of the Lord say, "No." My heart sank as I attempted to petition the Lord for this child's life, yet when I did I somehow felt as if the phone line had been severed. I cannot explain it but, knowing the answer was a super-natural *no*, I started praising God for what He was going to do through the loss of this child, and I simply asked Him to grant strength and grace to the Hubbell family, Carol in particular. At that moment I felt as if the phone line had suddenly been reconnected.

On May 12, which happened to be my wedding anniversary, Kenneth was delivered. A perfectly beautiful baby boy with a cherub face, chubby cheeks and all…yet he was lifeless. The cord had wrapped around his neck and little Kenneth had suddenly been delivered first into the Everlasting Arms.

Yes, we grieved. We grieved for a family as a family. Many of us who had been at that beautiful shower just a week before now mourned with a hurting family at Kenneth's tiny grave. A number of days after the funeral, when the Hubbell children were back to school, Carol's husband was back at work, and her extended family and friends had flown back home, a friend and I popped over for a visit. I sat there in amazement at how graciously Carol was handling every expectant mother's worst nightmare. She was communicative about her feelings and her loss. We sometimes cried, and sometimes we even laughed. Amazingly, she talked naturally and openly about her emotional pain, and oddly, how thankful she was to feel it. I will never forget her words: "The pain makes me know I'm alive."

As I listened, I thought of how, in so many situations in my life, I had stuffed my own emotional pain—with the result that, before giving my life to Jesus Christ, I had become a hollow shell. Sadly, I had mastered the art of keeping everyone at arm's length, especially when I needed them the most. It suddenly dawned on me that the woman I had come to minister to had unwittingly ministered to me. She had struck a nerve, deep and thick, and I sat in awe of my God and this woman of pure, simple, perfect faith.

"Why?"

How do we make sense out of what seems to be senseless? How do we make sense of the loss of a precious little baby boy? We cannot help but ask, "Why?" Why was it that this little baby came so close to the threshold of birth, only to never have the opportunity of drawing his first breath? Why? We turn to one another and ask, "Why?" And knowing we won't get very far with human wisdom, we turn to God and ask, "Why?"

As parents, don't we sometimes respond, "I'm the parent—that's why," or "Everything is under control—go back to sleep," or simply, "Just because."

But have you noticed that our heavenly Parent sometimes gives us the same answer, except He does it in a much more loving way? He tenderly replies, "Be still and know that I am God." And truly, as tough as that may seem, that is all we need to know.

When we think of pain and suffering and seemingly purposeless loss, immediately we think of Job. Job and his friends tried to reason through his loss and suffering. God posed question after question to Job, questions relating to His creation. God said in essence, "All right, Job, want to know it all? Here it is, since you are reasoning about what you don't understand. Contemplate this if you can!" Job was so over-whelmed with what God set before him that he realized his own folly in questioning an all-wise, all-powerful, sovereign Lord of creation.

It was as if God was saying to Job, "Job, this is huge, this is bigger than you. It has to do with My eternal plan. You're temporal, Job, and you think that way. I am infinite, you are finite—and if I even began to explain it to you, you couldn't handle it, Job. I am not going to give you every answer, but know this—not a sparrow falls to the ground that I don't know about. So how much more do you think I am concerned about those who bear My image?"

Yes, when Job lost his children, God said to him what He would say to you and me: "This is not *illogical*, what I allow—it is *a-logical*. It is not in the realm of your logic. It is beyond your ability to comprehend. Therefore, be still and know that I am God."

That is where Job came to have peace: trusting in the total sovereignty of Almighty God. How wonderful it is to come to the place of total trust, trust without question. May we link arms with Job and proclaim right along with him, "Though He slay me, I will hope in Him."[2]

His Will, His Way

Perhaps your fellowship is like ours. We offer baby dedications for new babies and their parents. It's not an elaborate thing, just a simple opportunity to make the proclamation that the intent of the parents will be to train up the child toward a loving relationship with God and that the congregation will support them in that goal. Before praying for the family, our pastor will ask a few questions of the parents. Not long ago, I asked Carol Hubbell if she and her husband would have had a dedication for Kenneth. Carol's quick response was, "Oh, absolutely!"

One of the first questions our pastor asks in the dedication is, "Are you fully willing to accept God's will for this child, no matter what?" I have yet to hear any parent say, "No," when asked this. Yet when God reminds us that He can take us up on that, that He can take what is rightfully His, many grieving parents ask, "How can a loving God allow such a thing to occur? Surely He could have intervened!"

The fact is, in general human beings do whatever they can to avoid pain. We seem to always want everything on our terms. "Lord, teach me this lesson this way, and I promise I'll learn it." "Lord if you get me out of this situation, I promise I'll..." "If you give me this job..." "If you heal my illness..." In other words, "I will only carry the thorn on my terms."

Yet in avoiding pain, we don't allow room for growth and maturity. Isn't it always a great blessing and encouragement to know people who've lived through horrible circumstances and then share about wonderful lessons learned, faith strengthened, families bonded, and commitments made to the Lord because of the horror they've suffered? Indeed, the valley of suffering can be a blessing—because it just might be what it takes to make us stop everything and reevaluate our lives, their value, and our priorities. Pain and suffering cause us to seek the answers to hard questions.

Simply because we in our finitude do not have the answer to the "Why?" question, just because we do not see the purpose for suffering, does not mean an infinite God does not have a purpose for it. I truly believe that God uses human frailty, suffering, and sickness to allow humanity to rise to the occasion, to bring out the best in those who bear His image. In all this He grants us the opportunity to reach out and love our neighbor as ourself and receive blessings that can only be perceived and appreciated through the eyes of the Holy Spirit.

If you have ever been close to those who suffer in Christ you will find they teach everyone around them that they can have a peace that passes all understanding in the midst of suffering. They are living testimonies who teach us that His grace is sufficient to take us through our suffering and trials. God redeems the circumstances that go along with living in a fallen world, and then He grants us an eternal perspective and an opportunity to lean on His sovereignty, to trust that He is merciful.

Yes—surely God could have intervened in the death of Kenneth Hubbell, but he had a greater purpose. Isaiah 55:8 tells us,

> *"My thoughts are not your thoughts,*
> *Neither are your ways My ways," declares the LORD.*
> *"For as the heavens are higher than the earth,*
> *So are My ways higher than your ways*
> *And My thoughts than your thoughts."*

Did Carol and her family shake their fists at God? Not once. Like the rest of us in our little fellowship and community, they watched blessing after blessing come out of a painful loss.

Human suffering does cause us to ask why a loving God would allow it. However, I know that God can and does bring good out of it. Again, in our finitude we do not see His whole purpose, but when we rest in Him and His attributes, we can rely on the truthfulness of Romans 8:28: "We know that God causes all things to work together for good to those who love God, to those who are called according to His purpose."

Keep Probing and Listen Well

Maybe you know someone who feels they simply can't put their trust in God because they agree with some of the challenges presented in this chapter. It has been my experience, as I chat with folks hither and yon regarding spiritual matters, that what I face at the heart of the problem of evil (sin, sickness, and suffering), is not so much an intellectual challenge as an emotional one. Thus, as women, I feel we can make huge headway in addressing this challenge. The reason why I believe this is true is because the topic takes an enormous amount of compassion and patience. Playing intellectual games in an attempt to win an argument will lose *any* witnessing opportunity, to be sure, but with an objection such as evil and human suffering in the world, the damage we may do can go much deeper. We can pound the table all we want, but unless we take the time to discover what is at the heart of the objection, we won't get very far in guiding the seeker to the appropriate answer.

I find that when I really take the time to delve into the reason behind the objection, a heart-wrenching story usually follows. The whole key is to grant individuals the opportunity to feel loved and safe enough to express their pain and anger in a noncombative environment. When I spoke with that angry World War II veteran, I reminded him of how gracious God had been to send him over to liberate those prisoners whom sick, sinful mankind had treated so horribly. After a short discussion, he acknowledged that at the very least there must be a God. He understood that the horror he had witnessed was not God's doing. God's doing had been to send him there to rescue people. It was wonderful to see his attitude toward God—and his countenance—change, but first, I had to take the time to discover the "why?" behind his anger. It was certainly worth it.

Final Thoughts

That we would have joy in this life at all is an amazing thing, isn't it? That we can feel God's presence as we walk among the thorns and thistles life seems to put in our paths is truly an incredible mystery. Hopefully, as your seeking friends and family watch you react to your less-than-ideal circumstances, whatever they may be, they will ask, "How can you have such peace? I know how I would react. What do you have that I don't?"

This is how God redeems our suffering. In the midst of it, we fulfill God's purpose for our lives. By His grace, and when we know we are in His will, at the very point of our suffering we can have strength, and wisdom, and peace—and yes, even joy. If, no matter what, we can have this joy here and now walking in His will, can you just imagine how much beyond joy it will be to fulfill our eternal purpose when we finally have the opportunity to see Him face-to-face and enjoy Him forever?

Yes, today we stand on this side of time and ask and wonder "Why?" But when He takes us from this life into the next, I imagine that our Lord will point to those who have been drawn to Him through tragic events and by His lovingkindness—and He'll say, "...him, and her, and them, and them, and all because of..." The Scriptures reveal that there are

things which eye has not seen and ear has not heard,
And which have not entered the heart of man,
All that God has prepared for those who love Him.[3]

While it will be nice to know the answers, somehow I think the pain we endured, the loss we suffered, the horror we witnessed, will be a faint memory as we stand in the presence of the Lord and those we love who have gone before us.

But until then we must live today, the day the Lord has made, no matter what it holds. We must live in a world where evil abounds, so what is the best way to cope? We not only cope but press on toward the prize through

• the support of our brothers and sisters in Christ

• the washing of the reading of the Word of God, which keeps everything in perspective and gives us the wisdom we so desperately need

- casting our cares at the feet of our Sovereign Lord through prayer

- reaching out to others and not fretting over our circumstances because God already knows all about them

Along these lines, please consider the truth and beauty in what Arthur Pink wrote in his book *The Attributes of God:*

> Seeing that He is clothed with omnipotence, no prayer is too hard for Him to answer, no need too great for Him to supply, no passion too strong for Him to subdue; no temptation too powerful for Him to deliver from, no misery too deep for Him to relieve.[4]

Questions for Reflection

1. *How did evil creep into God's very good creation?*

2. *What is the best way to help someone who is struggling with the problem of evil and human suffering?*

3. *What circumstances can you share that show how God brought good out of a bad situation?*

4. *What is humankind's usual response to pain and suffering? Why?*

5. *If you've been touched by Kenneth's story, would you please write me? Carol and I would be greatly blessed. Thank you!*

Suggested Resources

The Case for Faith by Lee Strobel. Zondervan Publishing House, 2000.

The Problem of Pain by C.S. Lewis. HarperSanFrancisco, 2001.

The Attributes of God by Arthur W. Pink. Baker Books, 1977.

PART THREE

It's All
About Jesus

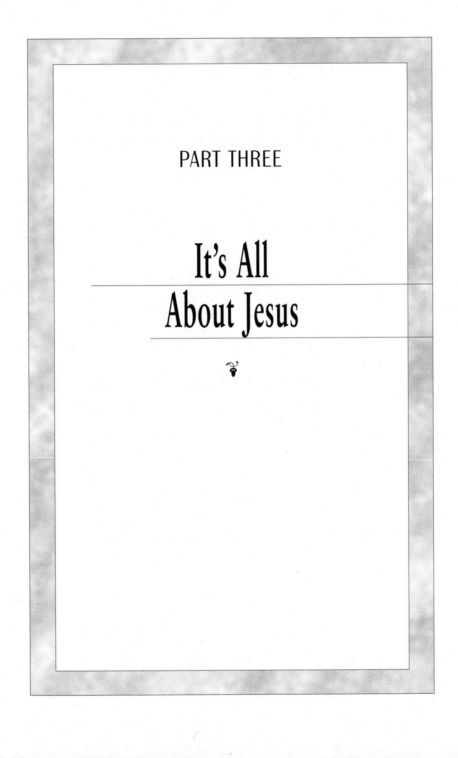

CHAPTER 7

Knowing That Jesus Is
Who He Claimed to Be

ave you ever noticed how, at any given time, some passages of Scripture seem to captivate your mind more than others do? It might even be a passage that had never really jumped out at you when you'd perused it in the past. Yet for some reason, it almost seems as if you are transported to that place and time as you meditate on the text. I've recently had this experience, and I thought I just might share it with you.

Now, picture if you will an exquisite chariot moving gracefully along an ancient road. The chariot, ornate and stately, offers a display of wealth and splendor. Its main occupant is a man of great influence and authority—he is a royal court official, to be exact. The man, with beautiful ebony skin and a strong voice, is seated quite comfortably as he reads the Scriptures aloud, perhaps to occupy the minds of his charioteers as well. He is the Ethiopian eunuch of Acts 8:27-39. Philip, a disciple of the Lord, was suddenly brought by the Spirit of God to the man's chariot and found him reading from the book of Isaiah:

He was led as a sheep to slaughter;
And as a lamb before its shearer is silent,
So He does not open His mouth.
In humiliation His judgment was taken away;

> *Who will relate His generation?*
> *For His life is removed from the earth.*[1]

This proselyte to Judaism, who had spent time in Jerusalem worshiping God, was prompted by this compelling passage to ask Philip the one question every believer desires to answer. "Please tell me, of whom does the prophet say this? Of himself or of someone else?" The answer led the Ethiopian eunuch to immediate conversion, baptism, and rejoicing as he traveled home to influence his own country with the knowledge of the identity of the Suffering Servant of Isaiah 53.

Now, while Acts 8:27-39 may not jump off the pages for everyone, surely Isaiah 53 immediately grabs the attention of almost every reader. There is something terribly compelling regarding the prophecy in Isaiah 53, just as there is something terribly compelling about the One who fulfilled it.

The Most Critical Question

Jesus asked the question, "Who do you say that I am?" For a long time, especially during my youth, my response might just have been that He was Mary's son, who for some strange reason I didn't quite understand was crucified under the authority of Pontius Pilate. That Jesus had fulfilled any prophecies—of this I was completely unaware. As far as ascribing deity to Him...according to my uneducated opinion, no one could really ever know a thing like that for certain.

Then, at the age of about 18, I had what I usually refer to as an "emotional experience in a church hall." The hellfire-and-brimstone message got me out of my seat and in front of an altar, desiring a ticket to heaven. *Repeat a prayer? If that is all there is to it, why, I can do that.* Two weeks after my lickety-split baptism, I asked the pastor a question after being challenged by a couple of unbelievers regarding my "conversion." (The unbelievers' goal had been to show me just how much I didn't know. It worked.)

Now, my question to the pastor was simple. But I never expected the answer I received. Surely the pastor would confirm my suspicion that no one could possibly know a thing like this absolutely, so I asked, almost flippantly, "Was Jesus God?" Thinking back on this, I wish I had had a camera to capture the somewhat uncomfortable and puzzled expression on the pastor's face as he slowly nodded in affirmation and stammered, "Y–Yes, Jesus *is* God." When I truly gave my life to the Lord Jesus Christ ten years later, the question of who He was and is was finally and completely settled in my heart, mind, and soul.

No matter how the question is framed, no matter what prompts it, it is the most important question anyone can ask, for the answer indeed holds eternal implications. Who was Jesus of Nazareth? Since He is the central figure of our faith, let's take a look at the person of Jesus, humanly speaking and spiritually speaking. Let's also take a look at what Jesus said of Himself and why He is to be believed—and especially why, at His name, every knee will bow and every tongue will confess that Jesus Christ is Lord to the glory of God the Father.[2]

Humanly Speaking, His Fame Makes No Sense

Who was this Jesus? Who was this man who has impacted human history more than any man who has ever walked the face of this planet? What was it about Him, that His name should still spark such debate and passion even 2000 years after His death? After all, even before His birth the deck seemed stacked against Him in regard to worldly fame and success, since His very conception appeared to be questionable. His place of birth wasn't a famed city such as Rome, nor some great palace—neither was His cradle a glorious bassinet trimmed in gold. Quite the contrary—He was born in a cave among rank farm animals—His cradle, a feeding trough. And, putting the lie to the depictions of a handsome Jesus with blonde hair, blue eyes, and European features, the Scriptures state that He had "no stately form or majesty that we should look upon Him, nor appearance that we should be attracted to Him."[3]

Jesus was not a famous conqueror of armies or nations, especially since He never traveled more than a hundred miles from His birthplace. He never attempted to achieve the office of governor, or mayor, let alone Caesar. As far as His teachings were concerned, many of the fundamentals that He taught about living life as it ought to be lived could actually be found in not only the Jewish tradition but among the ancient philosophers as well.

Unlike Paul, Jesus was not trained under erudite Gamaliel. Neither was Jesus a Pharisee of Pharisees among the religious leaders of His day, which would have afforded Him a platform for immediate success had that been His desire. Rather, He was a humble carpenter, plying His stepfather's trade—and his spiritual forerunner was His fiery cousin, John. To some, I'm sure, Cousin John seemed a madman—bellowing a message of repentance and baptism to all who'd listen, living in the wilderness clothed in animal skins, and surviving on a steady diet of locusts and wild honey.

Jesus, I'm sure, would have had no use at all for books like *How to Win Friends and Influence People,* since His words often cut to the quick. At times, His bold proclamations about Himself were difficult for even His own followers to accept, and "as a result many of His disciples withdrew and were not walking with Him anymore."[4] The core of His message did not tickle the ears, since it was not the wondrous glories of heaven that He spoke of the most, but the torment of hell and the horror of judgment.

Jesus' own siblings didn't take Him seriously, and they even seemed sarcastically resentful of His growing popularity.[5] He didn't take 20 years to establish Himself, building His fame through Madison Avenue sales-and-marketing techniques. He did not enlist the biggest and brightest Oxford scholars, nor did He call upon the likes of Anthony Robbins to afford His followers a you-can-do, coal-walkin' attitude. Rather, Jesus' ministry lasted just three short years. Of His companions, a motley crew of only 12 chosen men, one stole from the money bag and later betrayed Him, one denied Him three times, and all abandoned Him in His greatest hour of agony. In one week He heard the same crowd's shouts of "Hosanna! Blessed is the King who comes in the name of the Lord," turn to cries of "Crucify Him! Crucify Him!" And that they did.

Three Amazing Things

Even today, the utterance of Jesus' name incites more passion than any other ever uttered by believer or unbeliever alike. I will never forget a conversation I had years ago with a co-worker. She seemed to go out of her way to use Jesus' name as disrespectfully as you can imagine. Not knowing what else to say, I finally remarked, "I thought you didn't believe in Jesus."

"I don't," she replied.

With a grin on my face and an ironic tone in my voice, I asked, "Then why do you constantly call upon Him?"

She hotly declared, "I use His name that way because I hate everything He represents." The level of her anger took me quite by surprise.

So what is it about the person of Jesus that incites such passion either for Him or against Him? First, let's consider three rather important points that set Him apart from any other leader, religious or otherwise:

1. Jesus always spoke the truth.

2. Jesus lived perfectly consistent with God's high moral standards—not man's compromising, rule-bending standards.

3. Jesus said He was God.

Point number one and point number two are what made Jesus believable, so that when He proclaimed point number three, all honest observers were forced to take a serious look. When you trust someone, you usually don't have to question their claims. I could cite several good examples of this principle, but one in particular immediately comes to mind. It has to do with a rather puzzling mystery that we thought involved our daughter, who in the past had never made a habit of lying to us.

One morning, as I was preparing for the day, upon opening the bottom drawer of my vanity I noticed Q-Tips strewn all around the drawer, and most of the cotton was missing off the tips. Clearly, this seemed like something strange for my husband to do. Perhaps I had been snoring...and for lack of cotton balls, he had chosen the Q-Tip *tips*. I showed them to my husband, and after being as dumbstruck as I, he, along with me, sat down with our then seven-year-old daughter for the interrogation. In the past, if she'd been involved in mischief, her confession had usually been immediate. It had just never entered her mind to lie about her misdemeanors.

This time she was emphatic. We sat stunned as this child told us, with a straight face, that she hadn't done it. "Oh, so maybe Mikael did it?" "No," came her quick reply—as if to say, *How stupid can these people be? They know he's just an infant!* Then, at just about the same moment, my husband and I noticed something funny about the opening to the box. It was quite frayed. After setting several mouse-traps (welcome to the woods), we offered our humble apologies to our daughter, who maintained her integrity to the end. Knowing Nicole's track record of honesty had brought credibility to her claim of innocence, yet from our perspective the circumstances had made her claim hard for us to believe. We were wrong.

Again, though, when we consider Jesus' complete truthfulness and integrity (points one and two), His claims of deity must cause us to stop short and take careful notice.

God? Or Just Another Great Moral Teacher?

Whenever I read the Scriptures and reflect on what Jesus said of Himself, and then imagine anyone else making the same types of bold proclamations He made, I'm sure they would be fitted for a strait-jacket without delay. It's just that simple. I don't care how wonderful they are, they would be promptly escorted to their very own padded room. Consider the chat Jesus had with the high priest at His mock trial:

> *The high priest was questioning Him, and saying to Him, "Are You the Christ [Messiah], the Son of the Blessed One?" And Jesus said, "I am; and you shall see the Son of Man sitting at the right hand of power, and coming with the clouds of heaven."*[6]

See what I mean?

Now, I'm sure you've talked with folks who seem very reverent about Jesus as a good teacher, citing the Sermon on the Mount as an example. Indeed, they esteem Him as the greatest, most moral man who ever lived. Yet when push comes to shove, they stop short of calling Him Lord and God. However, if Jesus was not who He claimed to be, He could not have been a good teacher. Good teachers are not delusional—and Jesus would have to have been delusional if He were not God yet believed sincerely that He was. On the other hand, if Jesus was not God and knew He was not God, then He was not a good teacher, but a deceiver. Those are the only two choices—delusional or deceiver—if Jesus were not the divine Deliverer.

No one expressed this premise better than the great Christian apologist and thinker C.S. Lewis:

> I am trying here to prevent anyone saying the really foolish thing that people often say about Him: "I'm ready to accept Jesus as a great moral teacher, but I don't accept His claim to be God." That is the one thing we must not say. A man who was merely a man and said the sort of things Jesus said would not be a great moral teacher. He would either be a lunatic—on the level with a man who says he is a poached egg—or else he would be the Devil of Hell. You must make your choice. Either this man was, and is, the Son of God: or else a madman or something worse.
>
> You can shut Him up for a fool, you can spit at Him and kill Him as a demon; or you can fall at His feet and call Him Lord and God. But let us not come with any patronizing nonsense about His being a great human teacher. He has not left that open to us. He did not intend to.[7]

Maybe We Misheard Him

Perhaps you have also had discussions with folks who deny that Jesus ever claimed deity. I have met several individuals who've flatly asserted, "Jesus never said He was God." Now, not only would this come as a shock to Jesus, but also to the religious leaders of His day. After all, He was crucified for blasphemy.

Anyone who thinks that Jesus never claimed to be God has got to stop and think carefully after reading John 8:58-59: "Jesus said to them, 'Truly, truly, I say to you, before Abraham was born, I am.' Therefore they picked up stones to throw at Him; but Jesus hid Himself and went out of the temple."

Now, why on earth would the Jewish leaders of His day want to stone Him? Was it because He suggested that He was a good moral teacher? Perhaps there was simply gross confusion regarding His claims. Perhaps the Gospel writers and the religious leaders of His day only *thought* He had referred to Himself as God—which means His crucifixion was all just misunderstanding. Let's think about this for a moment. What did Jesus really mean when He referred to Himself as God?

Did He mean He was a Mormon—that He had become a god, and that we can too? Did He mean that He was one among many gods? Did He mean that, as the pantheists believe, that everything is god, and therefore so was He? Did He mean that through cyclic rebirth or reincarnation He had finally paid for deeds done in past lives and had reached a perfect state, but that He had just done it a bit quicker than the rest of us? Did He stand on a beach and yell, "I am God," as Shirley McClain did, and that's why He thought He had attained deity?

I don't think so. Everyone, from the Gospel writers, to the Pharisees, to the Roman soldier at the foot of His cross, understood perfectly what Jesus was saying of Himself. Most certainly, the Jewish leaders of His day knew that Jesus was identifying Himself with the I AM of Exodus 3:14. That is why they wanted to stone Him, and that is why He was crucified for blaspheming.

John 8:58-59 is not the only passage in which Jesus referred to His divine nature. In John 14:8-9 Jesus said that when we see Him we see the Father. His comment in John 10:30, "I and the Father are one," meant that in their very essence they are one unity.

Jesus was emphatic regarding the importance of belief in Him as He truly is, as in John 8:24: "I said to you that you will die in your sins; for unless you believe that I am He, you will die in your sins." There ain't no mincin' words there, wouldn't you say?

And in one of my favorite passages, Jesus disclosed who He really was to one of the most unlikely people. It is a true Cinderella story— of a waif who is met by, in this case, the Prince of Peace. Of course I am referring to the Samaritan woman in John 4. How many of us, as women who have made miserable choices apart from God, can identify with the woman at the well! Yet in her state of sin, and loss, and poor choices, the Wonderful Counselor reached out to her to reveal His true identity. "The woman said to Him, 'I know that Messiah is coming (He who is called Christ); when that One comes, He will declare all things to us.' Jesus said to her, 'I who speak to you am He.'"[8]

I could go on citing more passages, but I think the point is made. Jesus claimed to be God. So what we have thus far is a perfectly sinless life, a perfectly truth-filled life, and claims of deity. Let's take a moment to further substantiate those claims.

There's No Denying the Miraculous

It is sort of a shame today that so many common acts, as wonderful as they may be, are called "miraculous." Childbirth, for example, is not a miracle—it is not a unique, unrepeatable event. That lazy Joe got off the couch and got a job is not a miracle, it was a decision. That I finally got rid of that extra Christmas-fudge poundage from the holidays was not a miracle, it was sweat.

However, everything about Jesus was *truly* miraculous, from His conception, to His ministry, to His death and bodily resurrection. His life was marked by the miraculous. Even His enemies could not deny His miracles, but they attributed them to "Beelzebul," or Satan.[9] Nonbiblical writers of His time, such as the famous Jewish historian Flavius Josephus, wrote of Jesus as a miracle-worker. That He performed the miraculous is attested to in rabbinical writings as well.

There can be no doubt among the intellectually honest that Jesus performed miracles: bona fide, authentic miracles. He did not perform miracles simply to wow the crowd as did Simon in Acts 8. Jesus performed miracles to attest to who He really was and is and to confirm that He possessed God's authority over both the physical and spiritual realms, as shown by these accounts:

1. Jesus displayed His miracle-working divine authority over the elements:

   He got up and rebuked the wind and said to the sea, "Hush, be still." And the wind died down and it became perfectly calm. They [the disciples] became very much afraid and said to one another, "Who then is this, that even the wind and sea obey Him?"[10]

2. Jesus displayed His authority over physical laws, defying them, when He walked upon the stormy water:

   When the disciples saw Him walking on the sea, they were terrified, and said, "It is a ghost!" And they cried out for fear. But immediately Jesus spoke to them, saying, "Take courage, it is I; do not be afraid."[11]

3. Jesus displayed His authority over infirmities when He touched and healed the untouchable:

When Jesus came into Peter's home, He saw his mother-in-law lying sick in bed with a fever. He touched her hand, and the fever left her; and she got up and waited on Him. When evening came, they brought to Him many who were demon-possessed; and He cast out the spirits with a word, and healed all who were ill. This was to fulfill what was spoken through Isaiah the prophet: "He Himself took our infirmities and carried away our diseases."[12]

4. Jesus displayed His authority over the spiritual realm. And, as was not the case with the seven sons of Sceva spoken of in Acts 19, the demonic beings knew exactly who Jesus was:

Seeing Jesus from a distance, he [the demonized man] ran up and bowed down before Him; and shouting out with a loud voice, he said, "What business do we have with each other, Jesus, Son of the Most High God? I implore You by God, do not torment me!"[13]

When Jesus asked, "What is your name?" the man then answered, "My name is Legion; for we are many."[14] When the demonic spirits asked Jesus if they could go into a nearby herd of pigs, the Scripture states that Jesus gave them permission. Why did they need His permission? Obviously because they knew, since Jesus is Lord, they were subject to His command, power, and authority.

5. Jesus proved His authority over life and death by bringing the widow's son, Lazarus, and Jairus's daughter back from the dead.[15]

6. By His own resurrection (which we will look at in more detail in the next chapter), Jesus displayed the ultimate in power and authority:

For this reason the Father loves Me, because I lay down My life so that I may take it again. No one has taken it away from Me, but I lay it down on My own initiative. I have authority to lay it down, and I have authority to take it up again. This commandment I received from My Father."[16]

Jesus—The God of Abraham, Isaac, and Jacob

Indeed Jesus performed the miraculous. He indeed showed the attributes of Deity. However, does this necessarily mean that He is the God of the Old Testament, or rather, the Old Covenant? Are there any comparisons that would prove He is indeed the God of Abraham, Isaac, and Jacob? As my friend Suzanne would say in her very Minnesotan accent, "Oh, you betcha!"

As we know from our chapter on the existence of God, the God of the Old Covenant is omniscient, or all-knowing, "for the eyes of the LORD move to and fro throughout the earth."[17] Jesus, in His divine nature, is all-knowing since "He is the image of the invisible God."[18] "There is no creature hidden from His sight, but all things are open and laid bare to the eyes of Him with whom we have to do."[19]

Though He was not present, Jesus *saw* Nathanael under the fig tree. A stunned Nathanael announced, "Rabbi, You are the Son of God; You are the King of Israel." Jesus replied, "Because I said to you that I saw you under the fig tree, do you believe? You shall see greater things than these."[20]

Jesus was also well aware of the varied relationships of the Samaritan woman at the well. So amazed was she at His knowledge of her five previous husbands that she left her waterpot where she stood and ran back to her city, urging the men to "come, see a man who told me all the things that I have done."[21]

Supreme Spiritual Authority

Jesus displayed His power and authority to perform miraculous deeds as we saw earlier, but He also has the even greater power and authority to judge and forgive sins. Only God can pass eternal judgment and forgive sins, as stated in Deuteronomy 32:35 and Joel 3:12. Yet after Jesus healed the paralyzed man, He said to him, "Son, your sins are forgiven."[22] Now, notice the reaction of the religious leaders. When the scribes heard what Jesus said to the man they were angry and thought in their hearts, "Why does this man speak that way? He is blaspheming; who can forgive sins but God alone?"[23]

At this point I just have to shake my head. Here they totally ignore the fact that this poor soul can finally walk—that a miracle occurred right before their eyes. Rather, they rebuke Jesus for forgiving the man's sins. Talk about missing the point!

However, Jesus, knowing their thoughts (displaying His omniscience), responded,

> *"Why are you reasoning about these things in your hearts? Which is easier, to say to the paralytic, 'Your sins are forgiven'; or to say, 'Get up, and pick up your pallet and walk'? But so that you may know that the Son of Man has authority on earth to forgive sins"—He said to the paralytic—"I say to you, get up, pick up your pallet and go home."*[24]

In Isaiah 42:8, God declared, "I am the LORD, that is My name; I will not give My glory to another." In John 17:5, Jesus not only speaks of His pre-existence but states that He shares glory with the Father: "Father, glorify Me together with Yourself, with the glory which I had with You before the world was."

Further, Jesus stated very plainly in John 5:22, "Not even the Father judges anyone, but He has given all judgment to the Son, so that all may honor the Son even as they honor the Father. He who does not honor the Son does not honor the Father who sent Him."

We are to worship God and serve Him alone, yet Jesus accepted worship, unlike angels in a variety of passages or the apostles in the book of Acts. For example, after Thomas saw the resurrected Jesus in the upper room, he said to Him, "My Lord and my God!" To this Jesus responded, "Because you have seen Me, have you believed? Blessed are they who did not see, and yet believe."[25] Jesus did not rebuke Him—"No, no, Tom—you're breaking the first commandment—worship God alone,"—He accepted Thomas' worship.

A few more quick comparisons:

- Psalm 23 tells us that the Lord is our shepherd, and Jesus is as well, as He said in John 10:11: "I am the good shepherd; the good shepherd lays down His life for the sheep."

- Psalm 27:1 declares, "The LORD is my light and my salvation," just as Jesus declares He is the "Light of the world" in John 8:12.

- Only God can raise the dead as stated in 1 Samuel 2:6, yet we know that Jesus not only raised others, but Himself also.

Finally, a passage I just love to share with Jehovah's Witnesses, Isaiah 44:6:

> *I am the first and I am the last,*
> *And there is no God besides Me.*

Usually I will compare this verse with Jesus' words in Revelation 22:13: "I am the Alpha and the Omega, the first and the last, the beginning and the end." I will then direct their attention to what Jesus says to a terrified apostle John: "Do not be afraid; I am the first and the last, and the living One; and I was dead, and behold, I am alive forevermore, and I have the keys of death and of Hades."[26]

Questioning the Jehovah's Witnesses, I ask, "So, are there two 'firsts' and two 'lasts'? Or is one of the two lying? Or is the God of Isaiah 44:6 the same One who is speaking in Revelation 22:3 (as well as in Revelation 1:17-18)?" Since Jehovah's Witnesses are not polytheists (they would not acknowledge two "firsts" and two "lasts"), and since they do not believe that Jesus was a liar, then they must conclude that use of the same designation in both passages means that Jesus is God.

This is right about when they say, "Well, since you are going to believe what you believe and I am going to believe what I believe, it was nice talking with you—have a nice day." Since they cannot refute this proof of the deity of Christ, as with many people, evasion and escape are their only course of action. Sure, it can seem like I've just shot a BB at Mount Everest, but because I've given them the Word of God, I know it must actually be like an atomic bomb to an anthill. I never buy the façade. God's Word is indeed sharper than any two-edged sword, especially when it comes to the deity of our Lord Jesus Christ.

Prophecy Packs a Powerful Punch!

As I sit here writing to you, I can't help but wonder if you are as excited as I am about how rock-solid our faith in Jesus really is. Yet I have more to share with you regarding why we believe Jesus is exactly who He claimed to be. I can't end this chapter without looking at one of my favorite evidences for the fact that He is the long-awaited Messiah. In chapter 1, we saw how predictive prophecy substantiated the validity of the Bible. Well, it also substantiates our faith and belief that Jesus is the fulfillment of every Messianic prophecy of the Old Covenant Scriptures.

There are two powerful passages that I can immediately turn to in the Old Testament:

- Psalm 22, which depicted the crucifixion in detail hundreds of years before crucifixion was ever used as a method of execution

- Isaiah 53, the detailed description of the Suffering Servant

Here, though, I would like to look at a few other prophetic passages and leave Psalm 22 for the chapter on the resurrection (chapter 8) and Isaiah 53 for our chapter about the gospel (chapter 9).

I think you will find the time prophecy in the book of Daniel just as exciting as the above two passages. I have to tell you, every time I look at this passage I can't help but say to myself, "How could they have missed Him? How could they have missed the time of their *visitation?*" But, unfortunately the Jewish people did miss that time. Not long before His death, Jesus lamented, brokenhearted, "O Jerusalem, Jerusalem, who kills the prophets and stones those who are sent to her! How often I wanted to gather your children together, the way a hen gathers her chicks under her wings, and you were unwilling."[27]

And He sorrowfully warned in Luke 19:43-44,

> *The days shall come upon you when your enemies will throw up a barricade against you, and surround you and hem you in on every side, and they will level you to the ground and your children within you, and they will not leave in you one stone upon another, because you did not recognize the time of your visitation.*

Yet, whenever I shake my head over Israel, I think of myself as well. Do we not all have stories of missing His visitation? But back to Daniel.

Daniel's Time Prophecy

The prophet Daniel foretold exactly when the Messiah would come, in chapter 9 of his book. Now you can see why it is hard for me to believe that the Jewish leaders, who knew the Scriptures, would have missed their long-awaited Messiah. Yet this is also a fulfillment of prophecy. The apostle Paul explains this in Romans 11:7:

> *What Israel is seeking, it has not obtained, but those who were chosen obtained it, and the rest were hardened; just as it is written, "God gave them a spirit of stupor, eyes to see not and ears to hear not, down to this very day."*

Daniel 9:25 starts like this: "You are to know and discern that from the issuing of a decree to restore and rebuild Jerusalem until Messiah the Prince there will be seven weeks and sixty-two weeks." This is going to take a little explaining, but bear with me—it will be worth it! The context of the passage indicates that Daniel was referring to years, and one "week" in the vernacular of the day referred to one group of seven. After we do the math, it comes out that there would be 483 years from the time a decree was issued to restore and rebuild Jerusalem until the Messiah would come. Now the obvious question to ask is, do we know what year the decree was issued?

We sure do! As the Bible reveals and archaeology confirms, King Artaxerxes in 444 B.C. gave Nehemiah such a decree. (It's recorded in Nehemiah 2.) If you subtract 444 years from the 483-year prophecy and make the proper adjustment for the difference between the Hebrew calendar and today's calendar, we arrive at A.D. 33—not just the year or the week, but the very day Jesus came into Jerusalem on a donkey, which also fulfilled Zechariah 9:9:

> *Behold, your king is coming to you;*
> *He is just and endowed with salvation,*
> *Humble, and mounted on a donkey,*
> *Even on a colt, the foal of a donkey.*

Daniel's prophecy also stated that the Messiah would be "cut off"—die. One week after His triumphal entry into Jerusalem, Messiah the prince was crucified, making atonement for the iniquity of us all.

Jesus fulfilled hundreds of other prophecies concerning the Messiah. No mere human could possibly have manipulated circumstances to fulfill the wide variety of events. The probability that just 48 of these prophecies would be fulfilled in one person would be one chance in one with 158 zeros after it. That is a number that is almost impossible for the human mind to grasp. Yet by age 33, Jesus had fulfilled all 333 prophecies recorded in the Old Testament regarding the Messiah of Israel.

Prophecies by the Prophesied One

Jesus is not only the long-awaited Messiah prophesied in the Old Testament, but also the sovereign God of the universe, who made specific prophecies concerning individuals, events, and Himself. He predicted that Peter would deny him three times before the rooster crowed. In Matthew 24:2, He predicted the destruction of the Jewish temple. The temple was destroyed in A.D. 70, and when the dust settled, truly not one stone stood upon another.

Jesus also predicted His own death and resurrection: "Behold, we are going up to Jerusalem; and the Son of Man will be delivered to the chief priests and scribes, and they will condemn Him to death, and will hand Him over to the Gentiles to mock and scourge and crucify Him, and on the third day He will be raised up."[28]

Through His omniscience He proclaimed those prophecies, and by His omnipotence He fulfilled them. I'll let the Scriptures make the summation:

> *God, after He spoke long ago to the fathers in the prophets in many portions and in many ways, in these last days has spoken to us in His Son, whom He appointed heir of all things, through whom also He made the world. And He is the radiance of His glory and the exact representation of His nature, and upholds all things by the word of His power. When He had made purification of sins, He sat down at the right hand of the Majesty on high.*[29]

A Mystery: Two Natures—One Person

I think it is important to clarify one thing that I have made mention of in this chapter. A few times I have said, "Jesus, in His deity…" This brings us to another prophecy that I think needs clarification which will help us when we're sharing our faith with others who may find this basic Christian doctrine of Jesus' two natures a bit difficult to understand.

Isaiah 9:6 deals with this mystery and glorious truth, another difficult concept for our finite mind to grasp.

> *A child will be born to us, a son will be given to us;*
> *And the government will rest on His shoulders;*
> *And His name will be called Wonderful Counselor, Mighty*
> *God, Eternal Father, Prince of Peace.*

Now, how can one person have two natures? But there it is: "A child will be born," speaking of His humanity—but this child will be called "Mighty God." He will be born, yet He is the "Eternal Father"—eternal and preeminent over eternity.

This is the incarnation. God the Son, the second person of the Trinity, literally took on human flesh, human form. God became a man.[30] Man cannot become God or evolve into a god or gods. However, from the moment of the incarnation, Jesus was, and is, fully God and fully man. Peter Kreeft, a well-known Roman Catholic apologist, put it this way: "It is a mystery rather than a contradiction to say that He is one person with two natures, even if those two natures are opposites."[31]

However, we just might be able to grasp this when we consider that humans consist of body and soul, essentially two natures in one being. Jesus often spoke from the perspective of His humanity, referring to Himself as the Son of Man, and He also spoke from the perspective of His deity, as Son of God. In His humanity He was born in Bethlehem—in His deity "He is before all things, and in Him all things hold together.[32] In His humanity He asked Mary, the sister of Lazarus, where her brother's body had been laid to rest. In His deity He raised Lazarus from the dead with a single command: "Lazarus, come forth."

Jesus was one Person with two natures. It is just one of several doctrinal mysteries we believe by faith—and once again, we must take off our shoes for we stand on hallowed ground. *But why,* you may wonder, *is the incarnation an important doctrine for the Christian to accept?* Simply put, if Jesus was not who He said He was, then He was a blind guide and a deceiver. We are back to C.S. Lewis's "poached egg" comment. If Jesus is not God He cannot be Lord of all. If Jesus is not fully human He could not have atoned for our sins—He could not have been the substitutionary atoning One spoken of by Isaiah the prophet. And therefore, we would be without hope. It's just that simple.

Jesus in His Humanity

Jesus, as a man, is what man was meant to be. Jesus was consistently obedient to the will of the Father. He was consumed with a burning zeal to maintain the holiness of His Father's house, as shown when He drove the money changers out of the temple. His love for humanity was unconditional, for He laid down His life for the sins of the world. He possessed the heart of a servant, setting the example by wrapping a towel around His waist and washing the feet of His disciples...Judas included. Jesus was morally pure—as we saw, Pilate said, "I find no fault in Him." He was filled with compassion for the sick, needy, and poor...and along with those who mourned, Jesus wept.

Jesus Christ: fully God, fully man. Through His Divine authority He will ultimately judge the world—through His humanity He is the perfect Intercessor and Mediator for us before the Father. Since He is the One who created us, and is the One who became one of us, there is no one more appropriate and better able to speak on our behalf.

> *Since we have a great high priest who has passed through the heavens, Jesus the Son of God, let us hold fast our confession. For we do not have a high priest who cannot sympathize with our weaknesses, but One who has been tempted in all things as we are, yet without sin. Therefore let us draw near with confidence to the throne of grace, so that we may receive mercy and find grace to help in time of need.*[33]

Final Thoughts

When John the Baptist was imprisoned, he sent his disciples to Jesus to find out if He was truly the "Expected One," the long-awaited

Messiah and Savior of all humanity. Perhaps this account has been as much of a puzzle to you at times as it was to me. After all, it was John who proclaimed, upon seeing Jesus, "Behold, the Lamb of God who takes away the sin of the world! This is He on behalf of whom I said, 'After me comes a Man who has a higher rank than I, for He existed before me.'"[34] How could John proclaim His identity so boldly and then send his disciples to confirm it, if Jesus was indeed the "Expected One"?[35]

I think that question is more easily answered in light of John's imprisonment. Perhaps he was thinking, *How could this have happened to me? How could my situation be so hopeless, when I have put my faith and trust in the One who has finally come?* Yet, don't we all have our moments of doubt? Don't we too need the same confirmation as John when facing our own moments of imprisonment, whether they are physical, financial, or emotional? At those moments, I truly think our one desire is just to receive a reminder, a little something to hold on to. Jesus gave John just that—a reminder supported by evidence (as I hope I have done for you in this chapter).

Jesus told John's disciples to report back all of the wonderful signs He had performed, signs that attested to who He was. Then—and I just love the Amplified Bible's version of what Jesus said in Matthew 11:6—He reminded them that "blessed (happy, fortunate and to be envied) is he who takes no offense at Me *and* finds no cause for stumbling in *or* through Me *and* is not hindered from seeing the Truth."[36]

Were there more prophecies fulfilled than I've mentioned here? Yes. Were there more miracles? Yes. Were there more displays of God's mighty attributes? You bet. Therefore I conclude with the words of the other John:

> *Many other signs therefore Jesus also performed in the presence of the disciples, which are not written in this book; but these have been written that you may believe that Jesus is the Christ, the Son of God; and that believing you may have life in His name.*
>
> *...And there are also many other things which Jesus did, which if they were written in detail, I suppose that even the world itself would not contain the books which were written.*[37]

Questions for Reflection

1. *What two points made Jesus' claims believable?*

2. *Can you explain what the term "incarnation" means?*

3. *What attributes did Jesus possess that are also attributes of God?*

4. *Where is there a time prophecy detailing the year that Messiah would come?*

5. *Don't field mice just disgust you?*

Suggested Resources

Answering Jewish Objections to Jesus: General and Historical Objections by Michael L. Brown. Baker Books, 2000.

Answering Jewish Objections to Jesus: Theological Objections by Michael L. Brown. Baker Books, 2000.

More Than a Carpenter by Josh McDowell. Tyndale House Publishers, Inc., 1977.

Why I Am a Christian: Leading Thinkers Explain Why They Believe, edited by Norman L. Geisler and Paul K. Hoffman. Baker Books, 2001.

CHAPTER 8

The Reality of the Resurrection

𝔗hough this probably is more prevalent with the arts, isn't it interesting how people can see the same object or event, yet interpret what they experienced or saw quite differently? I guess there could be an array of explanations for this. One could be that the basis for their interpretation just might be their level of understanding and knowledge regarding what actually took place. Such was the case when I was driving into town one time with my husband and Nicole, who was then five years old.

Jeff and I, without acknowledging that we were noticing the same thing on the side of the freeway, glanced over but didn't react. I guess our feelings were similar, in that we wanted to avoid giving an explanation to our little girl, who was playing and singing so cheerily in the backseat of the car. Of course, nothing gets past the notice of a five-year-old. "Mom," she said excitedly, "I just saw three crosses on the side of the road over there." My husband and I glanced at each other knowing somewhat sorrowfully, it meant three individuals had somehow lost their lives. Seeing our saddened expressions, Nicole attempted to lighten the mood a bit by reassuring us, "Oh no, no, no—there was nobody on them." At this we were quite relieved.

From the variety of interpretations and perceptions of the event, I imagine the resurrection of Jesus Christ in much the same way. In my studies, I've read or heard everything from the idea that the resurrection

153

is simply "a metaphor of our own sacrificial self-giving,"[1] to the theory that it was simply a fabrication by an unknown, switched-at-birth twin of Jesus, who impersonated the risen Lord.[2] Everyone, no matter what their view—from metaphor to twin theory to hallucination to hysteria—can offer reasons why they believe what they believe about that first Easter morning.

However, the wonderful news is, as a believer, you can offer reasons as well. The question is, whose reasons are more reasonable to believe? That is the purpose of this chapter. Since the resurrection is the jewel in the crown of our faith, I want to make sure I present all the glorious facets of this jewel. What I'd like to do is break things down a bit—by using as a foundation just a few of the prophecies that were fulfilled in that one day.

In all, there were 27 Old Testament prophecies fulfilled in one Man in one day. Simply amazing, isn't? And isn't it just grand knowing that the resurrection of our Lord is so much more than metaphor? It is the redemption of our past, the reality of our today, and the hope for our tomorrow.

Now, let's go one step at a time through Jesus' betrayal, trial, and death—and the reason behind those dramatically changed lives that resulted.

The Pain of Betrayal

Even my close friend in whom I trusted,
Who ate my bread,
Has lifted up his heel against me (Psalm 41:9).

Judas Iscariot, who was one of the twelve, went off to the chief
priests in order to betray Him to them (Mark 14:10).

I'm sure you would agree that it has to be one of the most emotionally painful things to experience—not just the loss of a friendship, but betrayal by a close friend. Has it ever happened to you? Have you ever felt the sting of a false friend? Its wound can go deep and is certainly heartbreaking. If you have had such an experience, I hope your attitude was one of restoration—that, though it was difficult, you made an attempt to reach out to the individual who hurt you so. Jesus, forever our example, showed us just how to respond to those who wound us, even in the midst of their drawing the sword.

Jesus did not hesitate to wash the feet of His betrayer. After the foot-washing, that beautiful picture of how we ought to serve one another, Jesus let it be known that He was well aware of the evil plot against Him. "The Son of Man is to go, just as it is written of Him; but woe to that man by whom the Son of Man is betrayed! It would have been good for that man if he had not been born."[3]

Now, every time I read what happened next, what immediately pops into my mind is the old lineup. I'm sure, if you have more than two little ones, you've probably opted for this approach at your home as well. Just in case you are unfamiliar with it, it goes something like this: Mom and Dad, after gathering the children together, pose to them a scenario describing some sort of unexplained shenanigans by a mystery offender. Mom and Dad then wait patiently for a reaction from the peanut gallery. Usually the one who speaks most vigorously for his or her innocence is the guilty party.

This principle seemed to hold true at the last supper as well. After Jesus made His stunning disclosure about a betrayer, Judas immediately spoke up: "Surely it is not I, Rabbi?" Do you think Judas was just testing Him to see if Jesus really knew? Or do you think his conscience had not become completely seared and his own guilt prompted the response? In any event, Jesus replied, "You have said it yourself."[4]

Jesus not only assured Judas that He was aware of the plot, but He sternly warned Judas of the horrible consequences of carrying out his deed. Jesus confronted him, yet Judas's path was set—he was determined. Jesus let it be known that the one to whom He offered the morsel of bread was the one who would betray Him, and to Judas it was given. Once more Jesus reached out to Judas: hand to hand, and eye to eye.

The Scriptures state that as soon as Judas ate the morsel, "Satan then entered into him." How horrible that must have been. How incredibly awful it must be for those who dabble in the occult to be possessed by demonic spirits. Though demonic entities cannot possess a believer, how terrible it is to be oppressed by them. Yet

Satan himself entered into Judas and then led him to the chief priests and from there to Gethsemane.

"Do What You Have Come For"

When Judas was face-to-face with Jesus in the garden, an army of people behind him, he said, "Hail, Rabbi," then betrayed Him with a kiss. Then, in Matthew 26:50 Jesus called Judas exactly what he was— Judas, whom Jesus had chosen to be among His closest companions, who had witnessed His miracles and acts of love and compassion, whom Jesus had trusted with the money bag, though Judas helped himself to its contents. Jesus said, "Friend, do what you have come for." Now, whenever I'd read that passage in the past I had always assumed that Jesus might have been expressing some level of affection to Judas by calling him "friend." Once again reaching out would seem consistent with Jesus' character. Yet, according to *The Complete Word Study Dictionary: New Testament,* the word "friend" in Greek, as used in this verse, can be rendered "selfish colleague, friendly opportunist, or imposter."[5] Jesus again saw right through to the heart of the man and referred to Judas as an imposter there for the sole purpose of self-ish gain.

I can only guess, because it seems so like Satan, that after the dastardly deed of betrayal was accomplished he left Judas to himself. He left Judas to suffer the weight of his guilt and the certainty of judgment. Jesus' words must have been ringing in his ears: "It would have been good for that man if he had not been born."

Yet unlike Peter, whose denial times three brought him to a godly sorrow, then to confession and repentance, Judas tried to cover his tracks by returning the money. Perhaps he thought, like so many who attempt to make things right apart from God, *If I try to fix it myself by returning the loot, surely this weight of guilt will be gone and I will be absolved of any evil I've done.* He tried to do penance. It didn't work. (It never works, does it?) Judas knew that no act of his could clean the slate. Peter knew that no act of his could clean his slate from having denied the Lord, so Peter took his guilt to God and was promptly forgiven and restored, then used mightily. Judas, however, instead of throwing himself on the mercy of a loving heavenly Father, hanged himself.

I said to them, "If it is good in your sight, give me my wages; but if not, never mind!" So they weighed out thirty shekels of silver as my wages. Then the LORD said to me, "Throw it to the potter, that magnificent price at which I was valued by them." So I took the thirty shekels of silver and threw them to the potter in the house of the LORD (Zechariah 11:12-13).

When Judas, who had betrayed Him, saw that He had been condemned, he felt remorse and returned the thirty pieces of silver to the chief priests and elders, saying, "I have sinned by betraying innocent blood." But they said, "What is that to us? See to that yourself!" And he threw the pieces of silver into the temple sanctuary and departed; and he went away and hanged himself. The chief priests took the pieces of silver and said, "It is not lawful to put them into the temple treasury, since it is the price of blood." And they conferred together and with the money bought the Potter's Field as a burial place for strangers (Matthew 27:3-7).

The Trial

He was oppressed and He was afflicted,
Yet He did not open His mouth;
Like a lamb that is led to slaughter,
And like a sheep that is silent before its shearers,
So He did not open His mouth (Isaiah 53:7).

While He was being accused by the chief priests and elders, He did not answer. Then Pilate said to Him, "Do You not hear how many things they testify against You?" And He did not answer him with regard to even a single charge, so the governor was quite amazed (Matthew 27:12-14).

Have you ever been accused falsely? I think it can sometimes go hand in hand with a betrayal. Some time ago, an individual falsely accused me to others of saying something hurtful to another individual. I had no idea that for months this person had been telling folks close to me this horrible lie. It hurt deeply when I found out, and I was stunned at the people who had actually believed it. Apparently, it had been only after hours of long conversations and phone calls that someone had finally decided to ask the individual who I had supposedly hurt if this rumor was true. I was quickly exonerated. But I will never forget how I felt about the possibility that people I love would think me capable of intentionally hurting someone. This experience happened within a very small circle of individuals close to me—knowing that pain, I can hardly imagine how Jesus' heart must have hurt as He listened to those He came to save accuse Him falsely.

There stood Jesus before the chief priests and elders. His face was lightly stained with blood which He had sweated in the garden before His arrest. His anxiety and anguish had prompted an unusual condition referred to as *hematidrosis,* a condition which would also have left His skin fragile and very sensitive, only compounding the agony of the scourging yet to come. But there He stood before the same group who were so concerned with what was appropriate under the law regarding Judas' blood money in the temple treasury. However, they were perfectly fine with violating a myriad of other Jewish laws in order to rid themselves of the Man who threatened their very position and authority.

Illegal Proceedings

In *The Trial of Christ: A Criminal Lawyer Defends Jesus,* Dee Wampler wrote,

> The condemnation of Christ was not based upon legal procedure and harmony with either the Mosaic Code or the Mishnah. He was never legally tried and convicted. The pages of human history present no stronger case of judicial murder than the trial and crucifixion of Jesus of Nazareth, for the simple reason that all forms of law were outraged and trampled underfoot in the proceedings instituted against Him.[6]

What were these illegal proceedings? The following are just a few:

- The arrest was illegal since it took place at night and through the agency of a traitor.

- The private examination before Caiaphas (or Annas) was illegal because it was also conducted at night, and no judge, sitting alone, could interrogate an accused person.

- The trial before the Sanhedrin was illegal on several counts. It took place at night. The location of the trial was illegal. Jesus had no defense. Caiaphas presented the charge instead of the leading witnesses. No two witnesses could agree. Jesus was told to confess. The Chief Priest voted first by rending his robe and then immediately declaring that Jesus deserved death. Jesus was not guilty of the capital offense of blasphemy since He never pronounced the name of God (which could only be uttered once a year in the sanctuary of the Temple by the high priest).

Besides the illegal points of Jesus' arrest and trial, Wampler also cites a variety of trial errors. Since Pontius Pilate found no fault in Him, and Herod sent Him back to Pilate, essentially acquitting Him as well, Jesus should have been freed. He definitely should not have been scourged, let alone delivered up to be crucified. Yet it all followed a divine plan.

Delivered Over

Thus far Jesus had been, as prophesied, betrayed by a close friend and companion. He had then been arrested by night by a detachment of Roman soldiers along with the chief priests, officers of the temple guard, and elders. The rest of His companions had then deserted Him; one was even to deny Him three times.

Jesus, this Man of love and truth, of compassion and mercy, who brought healing and hope, then faced His false accusers. After this He endured the scorn of the crowds who had once adored Him, who almost rioted before Pilate was persuaded by their pleas to crucify Jesus and free a notorious prisoner named Barabbas. Jesus then endured the horror of a Roman scourging, a sharp, thorny crown pressed down upon His brow, and the humiliation and pain of being beaten, mocked, spat upon, and then prepared for death on a Roman cross.

Oh, what our Lord endured for you and me. Is there anyone on this planet any one of us would knowingly face these things for? Is there any secret we would keep if we knew we would face such horror? Is there any cause according to our flesh for which we would suffer such torture? All this, even before Jesus went to the cross.

> *I gave My back to those who strike Me,*
> *And My cheeks to those who pluck out the beard;*
> *I did not cover My face from humiliation and spitting*
>   *(Isaiah 50:6).*

> *Just as many were astonished at you, My people,*
> *So His appearance was marred more than any man,*
> *And His form more than the sons of men (Isaiah 52:14).*

> *Then he [Pilate] released Barabbas for them; but after having Jesus scourged, he handed Him over to be crucified.*
> *Then the soldiers of the governor took Jesus into the Praetorium and gathered the whole Roman cohort around Him. They stripped Him and put a scarlet robe on Him. And after twisting together a crown of thorns, they put it on His head, and a reed in His right hand; and they knelt down before Him and mocked Him, saying, "Hail, King of the Jews!" They spat on Him, and took the reed and began to beat Him on the head. After they had mocked Him, they took the scarlet robe off Him and put His own garments back on Him, and led Him away to crucify Him (Matthew 27:26-31).*

His Death

> *He Himself bore the sin of many,*
> *And interceded for the transgressors (Isaiah 53:12).*

> *Jesus was saying, "Father, forgive them; for they do not know what they are doing" (Luke 23:34).*

This might sound a bit odd, but every time I see someone wearing a cross I feel compelled to ask, and always in a very lighthearted tone,

"Is that beautiful cross you're wearing a fashion kind of thing, or are you totally sold out for the Lord Jesus Christ?" It is always fun to hear them respond with reverence for our Lord. There is instant fellowship, and I've met a sister or brother I will see again—if not in this life, in the next. But unfortunately, more often than not, the individuals I ask tell me they just like wearing the cross. They tell me they think the design is pretty. In other words, it is simply a fashion statement to them. How heartbreaking and, when you think about it, how foolish this really is. I often wonder if these same people would also wear a miniature noose, or electric chair, or guillotine, or some other method of execution dangling about their neck, in 14-karat gold, spotted with diamonds. Or would they, not being Jewish, wear a Star of David or, not being Buddhist, wear a Buddha around their neck or some other symbol of a religion they did not follow?

Perhaps you feel, as I do, that wearing the cross is a reminder of what our Lord suffered for us. It is a reminder that we are to pick up our cross daily and follow Him. But most definitely, it is the symbol of our victory. The cross we wear is not for the sake of fashion. And like the tomb, it is empty, He is not there. Jesus proclaimed total victory when He shouted from the cross, "It is finished." According to Zodhiates, the Greek word for "finished" means "to make an end or to accomplish, to complete something, not merely to end it, but to bring it to perfection or its destined goal, to carry it through." Zodhiates goes on to say, "'It is finished,' meaning the whole work of salvation, the very purpose Jesus came into the world."[7]

Charles Spurgeon once said, "What meant the Savior, then, by this, 'It is finished'? He meant, first of all, that all the types, promises, and prophecies were now fully accomplished in Him."[8] And that they were.

I will never forget chatting with a disciple of Sun Myung Moon on the subject of the crucifixion. She was convinced, as a result of her education through the Unification Church, that because Jesus was crucified, God had to resort to Plan B. That Jesus came to save the world, but they mistakenly crucified Him instead. And as a result we must now look to a new messiah to finish the job, the Reverend Sun Myung Moon. This was actually quite a surprise to me. I would never have imagined that the Jewish Messiah would be Korean.

Plan A: Prophecy Fulfilled

How truly fabulous it is to know that God never needs a Plan B. The crucifixion was nothing other than the fulfillment and culmination of every Old Covenant shadow or type. The particulars of the crucifixion were prophesied from Genesis onward. The crucifixion itself was, in fact, God's plan for redemption long before humanity even existed to contemplate the forbidden fruit. I could go into much detail regarding the prophecies fulfilled, but for the sake of brevity, below are some of the prophecies concerning just the events surrounding the crucifixion.

Dying Among Sinners

His grave was assigned with wicked men.
...He poured out Himself to death,
And was numbered with the transgressors (Isaiah 53:9,12).

When they came to the place called The Skull, there they crucified Him and the criminals, one on the right and the other on the left (Luke 23:33).

Bruised Heel

In Genesis 3:15 God said to the serpent in judgment, *"He shall bruise you on the head [crush your head], and you shall bruise him on the heel."* Crucifixion is the only execution method that "bruises" the heel. And the crucifixion was a crushing victory over the power of Satan.

Pierced

They pierced my hands and my feet (Psalm 22:16).

The other disciples...were saying to him [Thomas], "We have seen the Lord!" But he said to them, "Unless I shall see in His hands the imprint of the nails, and put my finger into the place of the nails, and put my hand into His side, I will not believe" (John 20:25).

Hanging on the Cross

> *I am poured out like water,*
> *And all my bones are out of joint.*

Psalm 22:14 is a picture of what happens when the arms of a crucified man are stretched and the weight of the body drops down. The shoulders dislocate, or go "out of joint." Since crucifixion is basically death by asphyxiation, Jesus would have had to rise up on the spike in His feet, thus bruising the heel, in order to inhale, then let Himself down again to exhale. Adding to His torture of having to move up and down on the cross to inhale and exhale was the fact that His back was torn to shreds from the buttocks to the shoulders as a result of the Roman scourging—a horror truly unimaginable.

His Garments

> *They divide my garments among them,*
> *And for my clothing they cast lots (Psalm 22:18).*

> *They cast lots, dividing up His garments among themselves*
> *(Luke 23:34).*

Staring

> *They look, they stare at me (Psalm 22:17).*

> *The people stood by, looking on (Luke 23:35).*

Taunting

> *All who see me sneer at me;*
> *They separate with the lip, they wag the head, saying,*
> *"Commit yourself to the LORD; let Him deliver him;*
> *Let Him rescue him, because He delights in him" (Psalm*
> *22:7-8).*

> *The chief priests also, along with the scribes and elders, were*
> *mocking Him and saying, "He saved others; He cannot save*
> *Himself. He is the King of Israel; let Him now come down from*
> *the cross, and we will believe in Him. He trusts in God; let God*

rescue Him now, if He delights in Him; for He said, 'I am the Son of God'" (Matthew 27:41-43).

Thirst

I am weary with my crying; my throat is parched;
My eyes fail as I wait for my God (Psalm 69:3).

My strength is dried up like a potsherd,
And my tongue cleaves to my jaws;
And You lay me in the dust of death (Psalm 22:15).

After this, Jesus, knowing that all things had already been accomplished, to fulfill the Scripture said, "I am thirsty" (John 19:28).

Offered Bitter Drink

They also gave me gall for my food
And for my thirst they gave me vinegar to drink (Psalm 69:21).

A jar full of sour wine [vinegar] was standing there; so they put a sponge full of the sour wine upon a branch of hyssop and brought it up to His mouth (John 19:29).

A Cry from the Cross

My God, my God, why have You forsaken Me?
Far from my deliverance are the words of my groaning (Psalm 22:1).

About the ninth hour Jesus cried out with a loud voice, saying, "Eli, Eli, lama sabachthani?" that is, "My God, My God, why have You forsaken Me?" (Matthew 27:46).

No Broken Bones

I can count all my bones (Psalm 22:17).

Coming to Jesus, when they saw that He was already dead, they did not break His legs (John 19:33).

Jesus, as John the Baptist declared, was the Lamb of God who takes away the sin of the world. Jesus was the final Passover Lamb, and one of the requirements of such a lamb, according to Exodus 12:46, was that none of its bones were to be broken.

Pierced

> *I will pour out on the house of David and on the inhabitants of Jerusalem, the Spirit of grace and of supplication, so that they will look on Me whom they have pierced; and they will mourn for Him, as one mourns for an only son, and they will weep bitterly over Him like the bitter weeping over a firstborn" (Zechariah 12:10).*

> *One of the soldiers pierced His side with a spear... (John 19:34).*

Brokenhearted

> *Reproach has broken my heart, and I am so sick.*
> *And I looked for sympathy, but there was none,*
> *And for comforters, but I found none (Psalm 69:20).*

> *I am poured out like water, and all my bones are out of joint;*
> *My heart is like wax; it is melted within me (Psalm 22:14).*

> *...and immediately blood and water came out (John 19:34).*

A Wealthy Burial

> *His grave was assigned with wicked men,*
> *Yet He was with a rich man in His death,*
> *Because He had done no violence,*
> *Nor was there any deceit in His mouth (Isaiah 53:9).*

> *When it was evening, there came a rich man from Arimathea, named Joseph, who himself had also become a disciple of Jesus. This man went to Pilate and asked for the body of Jesus. Then Pilate ordered it to be given to him. And Joseph took the body and wrapped it in a clean linen cloth, and laid it in his own new tomb, which he*

had hewn out in the rock; and he rolled a large stone against the entrance of the tomb and went away (Matthew 27:57-60).

Plan B?

The crucifixion of Jesus Christ was far from being Plan B. It was the apex of God's divine wisdom and sovereign plan. It was the ultimate expression of Jesus' love for humankind. In John 15:13 Jesus had said, "Greater love has no one than this, that one lay down his life for his friends."

When I think of the details of crucifixion—and I realize that Jesus knew every particular of what He would suffer, yet willingly faced it for me—how can I not fall on my face and call Him my Lord, and my God, and my King? Jesus told us that dying for a friend was the greatest expression of love, yet while we were at enmity with Him, He died for us. No greater love or compassion is there than His precious love for us, which He expressed unreservedly at the cross.

*Can a woman forget her nursing child
And have no compassion on the son of her womb?
Even these may forget, but I will not forget you.*
"Behold, I have inscribed you on the palms of My hands"
(Isaiah 49:15-16).

Ain't Nobody in Here but Us Linens!

They were on the road going up to Jerusalem, and Jesus was walking on ahead of them; and they were amazed, and those who followed were fearful. And again He took the twelve aside and began to tell them what was going to happen to Him, saying, "Behold, we are going up to Jerusalem, and the Son of Man will be delivered to the chief priests and the scribes; and they will condemn Him to death and will hand Him over to the Gentiles. They will mock Him and spit on Him, and scourge Him and kill Him, and three days later He will rise again" (Mark 10:32-34).

Now after the Sabbath, as it began to dawn toward the first day of the week, Mary Magdalene and the other Mary came to look at the grave. And behold, a severe earthquake had occurred, for an angel of the Lord descended from heaven and came and rolled away the stone and sat upon it. And his appearance was like lightning, and his clothing as white as snow. The guards shook for fear of him and became like dead men. The angel said to the women, "Do not be afraid; for I know that you are look-ing for Jesus who has been crucified. He is not here, for He has risen, just as He said. Come, see the place where He was lying. Go quickly and tell His disciples that He has risen from the dead; and behold, He is going ahead of you into Galilee, there you will see Him; behold, I have told you" (Matthew 28:1-7).

Have you ever been so entrenched in your valley experience that you could actually feel the thistle touching your chin? It's funny how we sometimes respond. We retreat, we withdraw, and we imagine the worst scenarios, ones that never come to pass. Simply put, we break out the double-dip chocolate-fudge-chip mocha almond rum ice cream and have ourselves a good old-fashioned pity party. And there we are, until the moment we see the hand of God move our mountain and then set us high atop His, so we can see from His perspective how the depth of our valley wasn't as great as we thought. And the moun-tain was of our own creation...well, it really was just a molehill after all. Our problem was actually twofold. One was our perspective from the valley, and the other was our lack of faith in God.

That's just where the disciples were, minus the ice cream, after the crucifixion. In the midst of their despair and the loss of Someone they had dearly loved, Someone whom they believed to be the Messiah, their pity party was in full swing. So when the women came to tell the disciples what the angel had proclaimed, and that the tomb was indeed empty, the Scriptures state that the women's "words appeared to them as nonsense, and they would not believe them."[9]

Peter, going into the tomb to see for himself, was not quite sure what had happened, but he "marveled." John's immediate reaction was unbelief, yet upon further examination of the grave and the posi-tion of the linen wrappings, and remembering that Jesus said He would rise from the dead, he then believed. Yet both simply went home. The empty tomb was not enough to move them out, preaching with passion and power. (And we all know Thomas's famous, perhaps even sarcastic, declaration of unbelief.)

The tomb was empty—no doubt about it. Even the Jewish leaders believed the terrified guards—they knew that the body was gone, that the tomb was empty. And they bribed the guards to report that the disciples had come and stolen the body.

Where Did He Go?

Now, I must grant the fact that an empty tomb does not necessarily prove that Jesus rose from the dead. An empty tomb simply prompts the question, "Where did He go?" Also, if the Roman guards allowed themselves to be bribed by the Pharisees, perhaps they could have been bribed by the disciples as well. Perhaps they were double-dipping. Maybe they were paid to turn their backs for a few moments while the disciples sneaked Jesus' body out of the tomb.

But would the disciples have attempted to steal Jesus' body to prove His resurrection? Is it possible that this would ever have entered their minds, especially since they were so skeptical regarding the testimony of the women? Would Jesus' followers, right after He had just been crucified for referring to Himself as God and King, then approach the Roman guards to ask for help in stealing the body so they could turn the world upside down with a phony resurrection story? Could they have said, "Excuse me, Mr. Roman Guard, who could be brutally killed if you left your post—hey, could you turn your head for a moment while we roll a 2000-pound stone uphill so we can make it look as if our leader rose from the dead?"

Can anyone honestly imagine those fearful, grief-stricken men concocting a resurrection story? After all, the disciples did not fully grasp the things Jesus had told them about His death and resurrection before He died. The concept of a crucified Messiah who would return from the dead was foreign to them, especially since they understood that the Messiah would be King. Therefore, as Jesus hung on the cross, their thoughts were certainly not, *This is how the events are supposed to be—He is paying for our sin, yet in three days we will see Him again!* No. They abandoned Him in the garden, fearing the same fate He would meet, and then despaired as He was laid in the tomb. But again, an empty tomb alone does not prove the resurrection. There has to be more.

He's Alive!

I think it is interesting that, though Jesus was a man of sorrows and acquainted with grief, with the cross ever before Him, He still managed to maintain a sense of humor. To the Pharisees He once said, "You strain out a gnat and swallow a camel." Pretty dry humor, but I think that that illustration is rather funny when you picture it. However, I especially wish I could have been on that road to Emmaus to eavesdrop on the conversation our resurrected Lord had with those two heartbroken men who obviously loved Jesus and were wondering why the tomb was empty. To paraphrase our Lord if I may: "So guys, anything new happen around here lately?"

The stunned men suggested He must have been a visitor, for everyone knew of the events surrounding the Nazarene. They then began to tell the resurrected Jesus what had happened to Him just days before. At this point, they were not aware that it was Jesus to whom they were speaking, for the Scriptures state that "their eyes were prevented from recognizing Him." The men were divinely blinded.

After they had filled Him in on the events of that weekend, Jesus filled them in on the whole picture. "He said to them, 'O foolish men and slow of heart to believe in all that the prophets have spoken! Was it not necessary for the Christ to suffer these things and to enter into His glory?' Then beginning with Moses and with all the prophets, He explained to them the things concerning Himself in all the Scriptures."[10]

Isn't that always our way? We try to inform the Lord of what He already knows. Finally, when we take a moment to put our emotions aside and are willing to listen and receive, when we begin to pull back from the situation and gain His perspective, suddenly we are able to receive the wisdom that's needed to pull us through—wisdom right from the heart of our Lord.

After Jesus had appeared on the road to Emmaus, He then appeared in the upper room to a group of disciples who, terrified, thought they were seeing a ghost. "He said to them, 'Why are you troubled, and why do doubts arise in your hearts? See My hands and

My feet, that it is I Myself; touch Me and see, for a spirit does not have flesh and bones as you see that I have."[11]

I absolutely love what He said next. It's just such a guy thing—and again, I think it reveals something of His sense of humor. Jesus asked His terrified followers, "Have you anything here to eat?"[12] Now, imagine being in the middle of mourning the one person on this earth that you most love. Suddenly, you hear something, so you lift your gaze from your sorrow, only to see that he or she is standing right before you. Do you think it just might break the tension a bit if they asked, "Hey, ya got any food around here?" Somehow, I really don't think Jesus was all that hungry. I think it was just His way of calming their fright, lightening up a pretty intense situation, and resuming the intimacy He had had with them the last time they had broken bread.

In 1 Corinthians 15:5-8 the apostle Paul documented other appearances of the resurrected Lord:

> *He appeared to Cephas [Peter], then to the twelve. After that He appeared to more than five hundred brethren at one time, most of whom remain until now, [are still alive to confirm this fact] but some have fallen asleep [have died]; then He appeared to James [Jesus' half brother, who before the resurrection did not believe He was the Messiah, but who afterward became a leader in the church and wrote the epistle of James], then to all the apostles; and last of all, as to one untimely born, He appeared to me also.*

This same Paul, on his way to murdering or imprisoning Christians, had met the risen Lord and as a result turned from the church's heartiest persecutor into its heartiest proponent. How does one explain it—apart from the resurrection?

Changed Lives

The apostles knew Jesus had died. Yet there He stood, flesh and bone. It was Jesus. Not a ghost, not a hallucination, not a fairy tale, but the resurrected Lord Jesus Christ. The apostle John wrote later about "what was from the beginning, what we have heard, what we have seen with our eyes, what we have looked at and touched with our hands, concerning the Word of Life."[13] The apostles knew what they had seen—they were eyewitnesses, and their lives dramatically reflected that fact. To me, this is the greatest evidence for the resurrection; the changed lives of the apostles.

Seeing the risen Lord changed cowardly Peter from a simple fisherman to a man who, by the power of the Holy Spirit, led 3000 people to saving faith on the day of Pentecost. Later, in Acts 4:13, the Jewish leaders marveled at the confidence of Peter and John as they stood before them, and they noted that the two men had been with Jesus. Peter, when in the hands of his executioners, requested that he be crucified upside down—which he would never have done if he had known all along he had bribed guards so he could steal Jesus' body.

In fact, each of the apostles—including Paul, who was beheaded—died a martyr's death. All except John, who, tradition tells us, survived being boiled in oil because of his testimony. Now, if Jesus had never risen, we have to wonder, even if the apostles hadn't died for their faith, what on earth would they have had to gain personally by spreading the gospel? Certainly by worldly standards they lost it all, especially Saul, who became the apostle Paul. Just listen to this account of the sheer glamour of being a witness for Christ during the early days of the church:

> *Five times I [Paul] received from the Jews thirty-nine lashes. Three times I was beaten with rods, once I was stoned, three times I was shipwrecked, a night and a day I have spent in the deep. I have been on frequent journeys, in dangers from rivers, dangers from robbers, dangers from my countrymen, dangers from the Gentiles, dangers in the city, dangers in the wilderness, dangers on the sea, dangers among false brethren; I have been in labor and hardship, through many sleepless nights, in hunger and thirst, often without food, in cold and exposure. Apart from such external things, there is daily pressure on me of concern for all the churches. Who is weak without my being weak? Who is led into sin without my intense concern?*[14]

I cannot fathom anyone deliberately going through those things for a lie. There was no other reason but that Paul—an intelligent, faithful Jew, a Pharisee among Pharisees—knew he had met the risen Lord on the road to Damascus.

Each of the apostles would have been able to share similar accounts, to be sure. Not one of them was willing to be silenced. Each one boldly proclaimed the most incredible event surrounding any human being in history. There is therefore only one conclusion: It is a small thing for an infinite God with infinite power to have raised Jesus Christ from the dead.

Final Thoughts

When talking about the importance and meaning of the resurrection of Jesus Christ, the apostle Paul was, as usual, very pragmatic. In 1 Corinthians 15:12-19 he wrote,

> Now if Christ is preached, that He has been raised from the dead, how do some among you say that there is no resurrection of the dead? But if there is no resurrection of the dead, not even Christ has been raised; and if Christ has not been raised, then our preaching is vain, your faith also is vain. Moreover we are even found to be false witnesses of God, because we testified against God that He raised Christ, whom He did not raise, if in fact the dead are not raised. For if the dead are not raised, not even Christ has been raised; and if Christ has not been raised, your faith is worthless, you are still in your sins. Then those also who have fallen asleep in Christ have perished. If we have hoped in Christ in this life only, we are of all men most to be pitied.

Simply put, if Jesus Christ was not resurrected, we are without hope. We are self-deceived and should be pitied since our faith was founded upon fantasy. But Jesus Christ did rise from the dead. He is risen! And because He lives, I can do more than face tomorrow—I can face death itself because it has lost its sting. I will live eternally with Him in glory with a resurrected body just like His, and so will you. We will eat, move from one dimension to another, all without the aches and pains of old age because our mortal body will have taken on immortality.

As we saw in the previous chapter, Jesus was truthful in everything He said and did. He was truly a good teacher—the best! Of the resurrection, He declared, "Destroy this temple [speaking of His body], and in three days I will raise it up."[15] Now, if He didn't raise His body as He said He would, that would make Him delusional or a deceiver and we are back to the conclusion of C.S. Lewis' poached-egg comment of the previous chapter.

In one of the best Christian apologetics books ever written, *Scaling the Secular City*, Dr. J.P. Moreland wrote this regarding the resurrection:

> The resurrection of Jesus of Nazareth from the dead is the foundation upon which the Christian faith is built. Without the resurrection, there would have been no Christian faith, and the most dynamic movement in history would never have come to be.[16]

Jesus said, "I am the resurrection and the life; he who believes in Me will live even if he dies, and everyone who lives and believes in Me will never die."[17] He was not delusional, He was not a deceiver—we are not blind guides, and we need no pity—because Jesus Christ is alive with power, and this is the good news we have the pleasure and privilege to proclaim.

Questions for Reflection

1. What happened to Judas after he ate the morsel of bread given to him by Jesus?

2. What did Jesus mean when He said, "It is finished." What was finished?

3. Can you remember three specific prophecies regarding the crucifixion?

4. Why do you think the disciples didn't believe the women's story?

5. Have you shared your resurrection account with anyone lately?

Suggested Resources

The Case for Christ by Lee Strobel. Zondervan Publishing House, 1998.

Christ's Words from the Cross by Charles H. Spurgeon. Baker Books, 1981.

Scaling the Secular City by J.P. Moreland. Baker Book House, 1987.

CHAPTER 9

Why the Gospel
Is Good News

will never forget the time I received a speeding ticket one fine fall morning as I was on my way to Bible study. While the other women got a real chuckle out of it, I was still trying to settle down from the adrenaline rush I'd gotten when I'd first noticed the red-and-blue flashing lights illuminating my rearview mirror. I'd been mortified when the police officer had cited me for speeding in a school zone. He had asked me if I'd noticed the 20-mile-per-hour sign, but I had to admit I hadn't. Later that day I drove very slowly through the area once again and could not find the school-zone sign the officer had mentioned.

When I received the formal ticket in the mail, I thought I would attempt to have the fine reduced to just plain old speeding. The fine for speeding in a school zone was pretty hefty—and besides, I didn't like being accused of trying to turn small schoolchildren into speed bumps! Wouldn't you know, about a week before I was to go to court, a brand-new sign was erected where there hadn't been one before.

The day of my trial came, and I sat nervously in traffic court feeling like an accused felon. Suddenly, the judge entered, and the words "All rise" echoed throughout the courtroom. We stood and waited respectfully for the judge to take his seat. As each docket number was called, the accused stood before the judge to plead his or her case. I was so nervous that my palms were actually sweating.

A hearty voice called my number, and I stood before the judge as I took my oath. With his glasses perched upon the tip of his nose, he fumbled through my folder as I pleaded my case. "Your Honor," I humbly muttered, "there was no school-zone sign posted on the day I traveled down that road." Nodding, he took off his glasses, closed the folder, looked straight into my eyes, and casually said, "Not guilty."

What! Did he say what I think he said? Maybe he thinks I'm some-one else. "You're dismissed," he said, then added with a grin on his face while gesturing gently with his hand, "and slow down next time." Still stunned, I thanked him and got out of there as fast as I could. I kept looking back, waiting for someone to grab me by the collar yelling, "Hey you...leadfoot...get back in here!"

The police officer had cited me for speeding in a school zone, but because the sign had not been posted at the time, my case was dismissed. In other words, what the judge had communicated to me was, "You are free from the penalty of your sin—now go and sin no more." What a feeling it was to have my debt canceled. What a wonderful feeling it was to have my penalty wiped out as if it had never happened.

Have you ever had such an experience? How wonderful it is that, as believers, we know the feeling of having the weight of our sin canceled at the cross by the Judge of the universe.

> *When you were dead in your transgressions and the uncir-cumcision of your flesh, He made you alive together in Him, having forgiven us all our transgressions, having canceled out the certificate of debt consisting of decrees against us, which was hostile to us; and He has taken it out of the way, having nailed it to the cross.*[1]

Jesus said, "Go into all the world and preach the gospel [good news] to all creation."[2] Truly, the message of the gospel *is* good news. However, the good news is first bad news. It is the bad news that makes the good news not only necessary but also the greatest news humanity can ever have the opportunity to receive. The bad news is why Jesus had to die in the first place—and that will be our starting point for this chapter on why we believe the gospel is good news.

First, we will look at our fall from the state of innocence, then the consequences of that fall. Next, we'll look at a temporary solution to our fallen condition, and finally, the glorious permanent solution and restoration before the Father.

The Gift of Life

When I think of God's love in creating humankind in His image, according to His likeness, my heart is overwhelmed with love for Him. Whenever I read the account in Genesis 1:26-28, I just can't help the emotion. God, like every parent, had wonderful aspirations for His children. They were to have dominion over all creation. They were to rule over the birds of the air, and over all sea creatures, and all land animals, and whatever happened to creep along our humble abode. They were to be faithful stewards of what God entrusted to them, and they were to multiply to the point of subduing the whole earth.

Best of all, this husband and wife would have perfect unity with each other and pure intimate love and fellowship with God. Oh, how His heart must have rejoiced over those He created in His image. Yet it must have been bittersweet knowing how hard they would fall. In the chapter on evil and suffering, I already addressed the abuse of the gift of free choice, so I want to look just a bit closer at what actually happened when our first parents fell from grace.

Chatting with a Snake in the Grass

You just might want to take a moment and read Genesis chapter 3, especially the part where the serpent charmed Eve. Eve knew that God's command was not to eat of the fruit. But, you know how good we are, especially as women, at justifying just about anything. "It's a gorgeous dress, if I don't get it now I'll miss the sale. I know our budget is tight and it's expensive, but when was the last time I bought a dress that really fit? Then I'll have something for that dinner we have to go to six months from now." Or, "Oh, just one slice of that four-layer carrot cake won't hurt. My diet...well I've been really good today and I even walked all the way to the mailbox this morning, I deserve a reward." I think we get it from our first mother. After Eve's little exchange with the serpent, she did not seek counsel from God or from her husband. Rather, justification for sin went into in full swing. Can you just hear her?

"How simply wonderful this fruit looks. Surely, God wouldn't want to withhold anything good from us. My, I sure am hungry. Now, why walk three feet to that tree over there when, oh look, all I have to do is reach my hand out and—*oops*. Did you see that? It just slipped right off the branch. I hate to waste it by throwing it on the ground, especially when, according to that friendly serpent over there, it will make me wise. Now just think of how helpful that would be, particularly since I am supposed to be your helpmeet, Adam. Oh, I know what God said, but that helpful serpent seems to think God's just trying to keep us from being like Him!" Perhaps it wasn't quite like that—but Eve didn't waste much time between gazing, and grabbing, and gobbling.

Adam knew the command of God as well, and the Scriptures state that he was with his wife when she ate the forbidden fruit. The serpent deceived Eve, and Adam did not intervene. Adam did not fulfill his role as leader and protector—rather, he listened to the voice of his wife and violated God's sole restriction.

And, surprise, surprise—the serpent had lied. Not only were they still unlike deity—at least in the way they had desired—but the image of God within them became marred. After they had eaten the fruit, notice what followed:

- *They realized they were naked.* Suddenly, something foreign entered their consciousness: shame.

- *Religion entered the camp.* Adam and Eve tried to hide their shame. They attempted to make things right by sewing fig leaves together for clothes, much like many do today, thinking good works or doing some sort of penance can save them. Adam and Eve tried to fix their shame problem apart from God.

- *They certainly suffered the loss of fellowship.* When Adam and Eve realized God was in the garden with them, instead of greeting Him and pursuing their heavenly Parent, they hid from His presence. I have to assume that God's question, "Where are you?" had to come from a broken heart. God knew where Adam was—to a far greater extent than we know when our children are in some sort of mischief. I believe the purpose of the question was to prompt reflection on the part of Adam on his descent from the estate he had had to the estate in which he now found himself.

- *They hid as a result of fear,* another thing totally foreign to them. They feared God, and to be sure, they feared impending judgment.

- *The blame game was in full swing.* Adam blamed his wife, then he blamed God for creating her for him in the first place. Eve said, in essence, "The devil made me do it." Then there was the serpent—but as everyone knows, he never did have a leg to stand on.

Adam and Eve fell from their state of innocence, which resulted in spiritual death at once, then ultimately physical death. All of creation suffered because of the free choice our first parents willingly made. Their desire was to be like God, knowing both good and evil. Their supreme desire was to determine, within their own hearts, right from wrong.

The Bad News

What a mess. Shame, religion (that is, doing their own thing apart from God), broken fellowship, fear, pride...I think our first parents got much more than they ever bargained for. Did you notice that there was no confession, no accepting responsibility for their sin, no godly sorrow leading to repentance? They simply covered up, hid from God, and then when all else failed, they attributed their sin to anyone but themselves. Sound familiar? This is the human condition resulting from the fall. The prophet Isaiah described it perfectly:

> *All of us have become like one who is unclean,*
> *And all our righteous deeds are like a filthy garment;*
> *And all of us wither like a leaf,*
> *And our iniquities, like the wind, take us away.*
> *There is no one who calls on Your name,*
> *Who arouses himself to take hold of You;*

For You have hidden Your face from us
And have delivered us into the power of our iniquities.
...Behold, the LORD's *hand is not so short*
That it cannot save;
Neither is His ear so dull
That it cannot hear.
But your iniquities have made a separation between you and
your God,
And your sins have hidden His face from you so that He does
not hear.[3]

It's a very sad picture, isn't it? And we are all guilty. Not one of us naturally seeks the presence of God. Rather, our iniquities move us farther and farther away from the intimacy of His presence. Have you ever noticed that the last person you desire to talk to is the one you've offended? Have you ever noticed that when you're out of God's will the last thing you want to open is your Bible? I know it's true for me. Because inside it lies conviction...and who needs to read about self-control or taking every thought captive when we're indulging the flesh?

The above passage also talks about God's face being hidden from a person caught up in the throes of their iniquity. The face is the source of blessing—and when we sin, His face is hidden from us. And it is not that God *cannot* hear when we call out to Him, but that He *won't*. I remember praying about and for things when I lived apart from God—and the non-answers I received I mistook as meaning that the phone was off the hook in heaven. That perhaps God didn't really exist, or that He was simply aloof.

But what I needed to do was forget my wants-and-needs lists and address what needed to be addressed: the fact that I was a sinner, lost and without hope. This is truly the bad news. How easy it would have been to keep denying these basic truths or keep trying to measure my righteousness or sinfulness according to mankind's standards. This reminds me of the following words of that great seventeenth-century preacher, Stephen Charnock: "Those that never had a sense of their own vileness, were always destitute of a sense of God's holiness."[4] Ouch!

God's holiness—the one element we most forget. God is holy and just, and as such, He cannot let sin go unpunished. The choice is, either wipe all mankind off the face of the earth or make provision for them. God, valuing those who bear His image, chose to make a provision. At the beginning, that provision for sin was simply a shadow of the final Provision to come.

A Temporary Solution

Now for the good news. God did not leave Adam and Eve in the fig leaves. (But not because they looked ridiculous and never would have sufficed for those upcoming cold winter nights.) God set a requirement to deal with their sin and shame…and that requirement has always been blood sacrifice. "The LORD God made garments of skin for Adam and his wife, and clothed them." [5]

In Exodus 12 we read about the first Passover. The children of Israel were to kill an unblemished lamb, which they would eat, but its blood they were to smear upon the two doorposts and lintel of their homes. When the Lord would see the blood applied to their door, He would pass over their home. The blood of the Passover lamb would save their firstborn.

The theme of the necessity of a blood sacrifice to satisfy the righteous wrath of God is all throughout the Scriptures and cannot be missed. Leviticus 17:11 gives us the reason for it. "The life of the flesh is in the blood, and I have given it to you on the altar to make atonement for your souls; for it is the blood by reason of the life that makes atonement." Hebrews 9:22 states that "according to the Law, one may almost say, all things are cleansed with blood, and without shedding of blood there is no forgiveness." Thus, the tabernacle and temple sacrifices were instituted for the sin of the individual, Passover was for the sin of the family, the Day of Atonement was for the sin of the nation, and the final Sacrifice would be for the sin of the world. This was the purpose of the Messiah.

A Picture of a Final Sacrifice

Nowhere in the Scriptures is there a more vivid picture of the purpose of the Messiah than Isaiah 53. Dr. Barry Leventhal, academic dean and professor at Southern Evangelical Seminary, wrote the following regarding his encounter with this passage as a young Jewish man seeking answers:

> I vividly remember the first time I seriously confronted Isaiah 53, or better still, the first time it seriously confronted me. Being rather confused over the identity of the Servant in Isaiah 53, I went to my local rabbi and said to him, "Rabbi, I have met some people at school who claim that the so-called Servant in Isaiah 53 is none other than Jesus of Nazareth. But I would like to know from you, who is this Servant in Isaiah 53?"
>
> I was astonished at his response. "Barry, I must admit that as I read Isaiah 53 it does seem to be talking about Jesus, but since we Jews do not believe in Jesus, it can't be speaking about Jesus." Not only did his so-called reasoning sound circular, it also sounded evasive and even fearful. There are none who are as deaf as those who do not want to hear.[6]

Take a moment, if you will, to read Isaiah 53. Included in it is a perfect definition of sin. The first half of verse 6 reads,

> *All of us like sheep have gone astray,*
> *Each of us has turned to his own way.*

This is the problem. Sin is the result of turning to our own way instead of God's way. However, the solution is found in the second half of that verse.

> *But the LORD has caused the iniquity of us all*
> *To fall on Him.*

There it is in one verse: the problem and the solution. As we read this entire passage of Scripture, we cannot help but recognize the prophecies as fulfilled in Jesus. The Servant would, according to verse 10, "render Himself as a guilt offering." Not only that, but this Servant would also render Himself up willingly.

The final perfect picture of the atonement is found in verse 11:

> *As a result of the anguish of His soul,*
> *He will see it and be satisfied;*
> *By His knowledge the Righteous One,*

My Servant, will justify the many,
As He will bear their iniquities.

In other words, God would see this guilt offering as a satisfactory, substitutionary, atoning sacrifice. The Servant of Isaiah 53 would bear the sin of others upon Himself, thus obtaining their justification before God.

Yet the good news keeps getting better:

Therefore, I will allot Him a portion with the great,
And He will divide the booty with the strong;
Because He poured out Himself to death,
And was numbered with the transgressors;
Yet He Himself bore the sin of many
And interceded for the transgressors.[7]

He will intercede on our behalf. He will mediate on the part of fallen, broken humanity. Is it any wonder why the Old Covenant saints longed for the Messiah? All the sacrifices of the Old Covenant were but a shadow of the fulfillment, the final sacrifice yet to come.

The Glorious Fulfillment

Jesus said, "Do not think that I came to abolish the Law or the Prophets; I did not come to abolish but to fulfill."[8] It really saddens me to think of just how many professing Christians there are who are unfamiliar with the Old Testament. I'm sure you can see how vitally important a knowledge of the Old Testament is for understanding the gospel message and why Jesus had to die, why He had to shed His blood. All of the Old Testament passages we've read thus far help us to understand New Testament—or rather, New Covenant—passages like Hebrews 10:11-25:

We have been sanctified [set apart] through the offering of
the body of Jesus Christ once for all.
Every priest stands daily ministering and offering time after
time the same sacrifices, which can never take away sins; but He,
having offered one sacrifice for sins for all time, sat down at the
right hand of God.[9]

> *The Holy Spirit testifies to us; for after saying,*
> *"This is the covenant that I will make with them*
> *After those days, says the Lord:*
> *'I will put My laws upon their heart,*
> *And on their mind I will write them,'"*
> *He then says,*
> *"And their sins and their lawless deeds I will remember*
>   *no more."*
> *Now where there is forgiveness of these things, there is*
>   *no longer any offering for sin.*[10]

Thus, with the atoning sacrifice of Jesus Christ—the final Passover lamb, the Lamb of God who takes away the sin of the world—the sacrificial system for sin came to an end. Jesus Christ died on the cross once and for all. To use the words of our Lord from the cross—"It is finished." Death, the penalty for sin, was conquered at the resurrection. The resurrection of Jesus Christ broke Satan's power over death. This is why Jesus had to die—so that in rising from the dead He would overcome the final penalty for sin.

Arthur W. Pink, an itinerant Bible teacher of the early 1900s, wrote,

> God's holiness is manifested at the Cross. Wondrously and yet most solemnly does the Atonement display God's infinite holiness and abhorrence of sin. How hateful must sin be to God for Him to punish it to its utmost deserts when it was imputed to His Son![11]

No More Separation

The moment Jesus died on the cross, the veil in the temple was torn in two from top to bottom, as we read in Matthew 27:51. No longer would the congregation be separated from the Holy of Holies and the presence of God. Jesus Christ took the penalty of our sins upon Himself and restored our intimate communion with the Father. So great was that final sacrifice on the cross that those who figuratively apply the blood of the Lamb of God to the doorposts of their heart are cleansed from their sin, saved from sin's penalty, and given access to the presence of the Holy Father.

At the cross the ultimate in divine justice was satisfied, and the ultimate in divine love was expressed as the ultimate penalty was paid for the sins of the world. As Savior, Jesus is the Lamb of God, who willingly offered Himself to pay a debt the world could never pay. While we were still sinners, while we were still enemies of God, Jesus Christ died for us:

> *By this the love of God was manifested in us, that God has sent His only begotten Son into the world so that we might live through Him. In this is love, not that we loved God, but that He loved us and sent His Son to be the propitiation [the required satisfaction] for our sins.*[12]

The restoration of fellowship, image, and right standing can only be found in the work of Christ upon the cross. Made in His image spiritually, though that spiritual image is marred by sin, we now have an opportunity to be conformed to the image of His Son and our Savior, Jesus Christ.

Believe and Receive

Romans 6:23 is a wonderful summation of the gospel message: "The wages of sin is death, but the free gift of God is eternal life in Christ Jesus our Lord." That seems simple enough. But how did we receive this free gift? Romans 10:8-10 explains just how:

> *"The word is near you, in your mouth and in your heart"—that is, the word of faith which we are preaching, that if you confess with your mouth Jesus as Lord, and believe in your heart that God raised Him from the dead, you will be saved; for with the heart a person believes, resulting in righteousness, and with the mouth he confesses, resulting in salvation.*

By faith, we verbally confessed Jesus Christ as our Lord—and the result of believing that God raised Him from the dead is a life change toward righteousness. We have been saved by God's grace through faith in the resurrection of Jesus Christ, and we acknowledge Him as Lord and Savior of our lives.

Now, what kind of belief or faith is this that we possess? It is a faith built upon a bedrock of fact. It is a faith built upon what you've read throughout this book. How unfortunate it is that many people quote Hebrews 11:1—"Now faith is the assurance of things hoped for, the conviction of things not seen"—almost as if this verse indicates that the faith a believer proclaims is simply a blind faith. Thankfully, our belief that the gospel is good news and our faith in the Lord Jesus Christ are far from being blind. God does not want us to believe in ignorance since His Word commands us to "examine everything carefully; hold fast to that which is good."[13]

Spiros Zodhiates defines the Greek word for "faith" used in Hebrews 11:1 and Romans 10:8 as follows: "That persuasion is not the outcome of imagination but is based on fact, such as the reality of the resurrection of Christ (1 Cor. 15), and as such it becomes the basis of realistic hope."[14] Isn't that wonderful? "Based on fact...the reality of the resurrection of Christ." We have faith in God not based upon sentiment or emotion but upon the verifiable fact that He raised Jesus Christ from the dead.

I think that if I had to base my faith upon my emotions I would doubt my salvation constantly. Some moments I feel particularly saved—like when I am sharing Christ with a seeker. However, at other times my hurried or grumpy mood may prompt not only me but others to doubt my salvation as well. But how many times have we heard unbelievers, after expressing their particular spiritual idea, defend it by saying, "I just feel it's true" or, "It just feels right." Now, everyone raise your hand who has ever been led astray by emotions or *feelings*. Fear. Pride. Anger. Lust. Depression. How wonderful it is to know that no matter how you or I *feel*, God did indeed raise His Son from the grave.

An Opportunity for Everyone

Jesus is indeed the Jewish Messiah, but not for Jew only. He is the Messiah to the Gentile as well. Matthew, applying Isaiah 42 to Jesus, wrote,

> *Behold, My servant whom I have chosen;*
> *My beloved in whom My soul is well-pleased;*
> *I will put My spirit upon Him,*
> *And He shall proclaim justice to the Gentiles.*
> *...And in His name the Gentiles will hope.*[15]

Hope for Jew and Gentile alike. "For there is no distinction between Jew and Greek [Gentile]; for the same Lord is Lord of all, abounding in riches for all who call upon Him; for 'Whoever will call upon the name of the Lord will be saved.'"[16]

Every human being on this planet has an opportunity to respond to God. The Scriptures appeal to us, if we hear His voice today, to not harden our hearts. We are to respond. He is compassionate and long-suffering. He is a God who said, as quoted by the apostle Paul, "All the day long I have stretched out My hands to a disobedient and obstinate people."[17]

When I think of my years apart from Him, I can see now how often He stretched out His loving hands to me. Yet all I did, to my shame, was slap them back. Perhaps you have a similar testimony as well. All of us—including me—like sheep have gone astray. How wonderful it is that He never gave up on us. He simply kept reaching out until we responded to His love.

Children of God

Along with the gift of eternal life through our Lord and Savior Jesus Christ comes a magnificent change in position—a change in our eternal standing before the Father. When we received His free gift of salvation, that was truly the moment we became children of God. "As many as received Him, to them He gave the right to become children of God, even to those who believe in His name, who were born, not of blood nor of the will of the flesh nor of the will of man, but of God."[18]

Now some might argue that all humans are God's children. However, I think it is important that we consider this concept in light of what the Scriptures state and not what tickles our ears. I'm sure you have, just as much as I, received e-mail messages from believers and unbelievers alike with what on the surface might sound good, but is actually quite heretical in its concept of what a child of God is. Consider the following message I once received:

> Make a wish before you read this poem. Did you make a wish? If you don't make a wish, it won't come true. Last chance to make a wish. FOR TODAY AND EVERYDAY. May today there be peace within YOU. May you trust your highest power that you are exactly

where you are meant to be. May you not forget the infinite possibilities that are born of faith. May you use those gifts that you have received, and pass on the love that has been given to you. May you be content knowing you are a child of God. Let this presence settle into your bones and allow your soul the freedom to sing, dance, and to bask in the sun, it is there for each and everyone of you. Send this to seven people within the next five minutes and your wish will come true. Hope you're having a great day!!!

Though I was one of the seven who received this message, I never did find out if the sender's wish came true. How thankful I am that our faith and relationship with God, and the blessings He bestows, are not the result of making a wish or sending an e-mail. Though this message has a quip about God, its essence is wholly of self. These types of e-mails and this type of thinking break my heart and, unfortunately, they are so prevalent. All too often, people think that simply because something has the word *God* in it, it must be true—it must portray God and how we can approach Him accurately. How sad for the author of the above message to have reduced God to a lucky charm.

Now, did you notice that the one mention of God was not really about God, but about the recipient? "Be content knowing that you are a child of God." How sad it is that a beautiful gift from God, the gift of spiritual adoption that we received as believers, is so often perverted to reinforce mankind's desire to do his or her own thing.

The Need for Rebirth

The Bible speaks plainly about who God's children really are. Paul writes in Ephesians 2 that when we were apart from God we were, by nature, children of wrath who walked according to the lusts of our flesh and of our mind. In the parable of the seeds and the weeds, Jesus referred to the good seeds as the sons of the kingdom, and the weeds as the sons of the evil one.[19] The apostle John wrote in 1 John 3:10, "By this the children of God and the children of the devil are obvious: anyone who does not practice righteousness is not of God, nor the one who does not love his brother."

We were once born of flesh by earthly parents, but we were born again in Christ, at which time we became children of God. In His conversation with Nicodemus, a ruler of the Jewish people, Jesus said, "Truly, truly, I say to you, unless one is born again he cannot see the kingdom of God."[20] Like many, Nicodemus had a difficult time receiving this spiritual truth, the truth of spiritual rebirth. Jesus explained, "That which is born of the flesh is flesh, and that which is born of the Spirit is spirit. Do not be amazed that I said to you, 'You must be born again.'"[21]

Unlike Nicodemus, the apostle Peter had grasped this truth. He explains it in 1 Peter 1:22-23:

> *Since you have in obedience to the truth purified your souls for a sincere love of the brethren, fervently love one another from the heart, for you have been born again not of seed which is perishable but imperishable, that is, through the living and abiding word of God.*

Isn't it marvelous that when you become a true child of the living God, it means that "you have not received a spirit of slavery leading to fear again, but you have received a spirit of adoption as sons by which we cry out, 'Abba! Father!'"[22] The word *Abba* means that you can literally cry out to God as "Father, my Father!"

Perhaps you're talking with a friend whose concept of God is perverted by an alcoholic or otherwise abusive earthly father. The alarming number of deadbeat dads and absentee fathers and the growing number of single moms leave fatherless children with one place to turn to for the idea of what a father is—and that's television. Sadly, we've gone from *Father Knows Best* to *Father Knows Nothing*. If a father is there at all, all too often he is portrayed as a bumbling fool.

Therefore, the idea of God as a male figure is tough enough, but as *Father*—well, that can be a major stumbling block. If this is the case, explain to your hurting friend that, unlike an earthly father who can fail or disappoint her, our blessed heavenly Father, who never changes, is always there to listen compassionately and lovingly to her heart's cry.

In *Knowing God*, J.I. Packer explained our adopted relationship to our Father superbly:

> There are no distinctions of affection in the divine family. We are all loved just as fully as Jesus is loved. It is like a fairy story—the

reigning monarch adopts waifs and strays to make princes of them. But, praise God, it is not a fairy story: it is a hard and solid fact, founded on the bedrock of free and sovereign grace. This, and nothing less than this, is what adoption means. No wonder John cries, *"Behold, what manner of love!"* When once you understand adoption, your heart will cry the same.

…If God in love has made Christians His children, and if He is perfect as a Father, two things would seem to follow, in the nature of the case.

First, the family relationship must be an abiding one, lasting forever. Perfect parents do not cast off their children. Christians may act the prodigal, but God will not cease to act the prodigal's father.

Second, God will go out of His way to make His children feel His love for them and know their privilege and security as members of His family. Adopted children need assurance that they belong, and a perfect parent will not withhold it.[23]

I think that this is almost too wonderful to grasp. God draws us to Himself by His loving-kindness, and then we have an opportunity to choose either to remain children of wrath, at enmity with Him—or to cry "Abba, Father" and receive the Spirit of adoption as His own child. Oh, what a precious thing! God loves us with an everlasting love and grants us perfect assurance, turning poor waifs into wealthy heirs in His glorious kingdom.

Final Thoughts

It is a trustworthy statement, deserving full acceptance, that Christ Jesus came into the world to save sinners, among whom I am foremost of all. Yet for this reason I found mercy, so that in me as the foremost, Jesus Christ might demonstrate His perfect patience as an example for those who would believe in Him for eternal life.[24]

Have you ever felt like the foremost sinner of all? Oh, how the enemy of your soul would like to convince you that you are without hope! "Blew it again, didn't you?" he whispers in your ear. But you have an advocate with the Father, Jesus Christ your Lord.

How wonderful it is to know that Jesus now speaks on our behalf because, by God's enormous grace, we have forgiveness. Perhaps Stephen Charnock summed up this sentiment best when he wrote,

> Without sin the creature [would] not [have] been miserable: had man remained innocent, [he would] not [have] been the subject of punishment; and without the creature's misery, God's mercy in sending His Son to save His enemies could not have appeared. *The abundance of sin is a passive occasion for God to manifest the abundance of His grace.*[25]

Now, while we don't go right ahead and willingly give God an opportunity to manifest the abundance of His grace, isn't it wonderful to know our sins are forgiven and forgotten upon the moment of our repentance?

God's abundant grace. Ephesians 2:8 reminds us it is by God's grace that we are saved from our sins and the wrath of God's judgment. Salvation came to us through faith, as a gift of God—not according to our works, which would prompt our boasting, "Isn't God lucky to have me?" But in humility, recognizing our need, we bow before the throne of grace and accept it. Oh, how hard it is for sinful mankind to bow the knee and admit the need! We fell in pride, and we continue our lost state in pride, for salvation comes by a willful act of humility before God.

I am continually amazed at how many people I speak with, whose questions are answered to their satisfaction, refuse to believe. As I mentioned in a previous chapter, the answers we offer simply remove obstacles to the conversion of the soul. Yet some will never believe, even if One rises from the dead. Nonetheless, never stop sharing the good news, and certainly never stop praying for them. Gamaliel had it right in Acts 5:34-39. If the message preached is of men it will eventually come to nothing—however, if it is of God nothing can stop it and those who fight against it will find themselves fighting God.

How tragic it is that many people would rather fight God than bow the knee. Yet bow the knee they will. Philippians 2:6-11 tells us that Jesus,

> *Although He existed in the form of God, did not regard equality with God a thing to be grasped, but emptied Himself,*

taking the form of a bond-servant, and being made in the likeness of men. Being found in appearance as a man, He humbled Himself by becoming obedient to the point of death, even death on a cross. For this reason also, God highly exalted Him, and bestowed on Him the name which is above every name, so that at the name of Jesus every knee will bow, of those who are in heaven and on earth and under the earth, and that every tongue will confess that Jesus Christ is Lord, to the glory of God the Father.

Are you sharing the Lord with someone you love who refuses to believe? Never stop bending your knee and praying on their behalf that the Lord would soften their heart to receive Him before it's too late.

One last thought. Lest we ever forget what our Lord and Savior Jesus Christ saved us from, consider for a moment something called the "sin tax." In case you are unfamiliar, a sin tax is basically a sales tax tacked onto vices such as alcohol and cigarettes. Now, can you imagine if there really were a tax for each and every one of our sins, sins we've committed in thought and deed? We would, each one of us, find ourselves in debtor's prison, which I suppose would be more commonly known as hell.

However, Jesus left the glories of heaven to become a man. He suffered at the hands of sinful mankind and died to pay our sin tax upon the cross—a price impossible for us to pay. He then rose from the dead, conquering the ultimate penalty for sin and thus freeing us from bondage to the enemy of our soul. And when all is said and done in this life, we will praise Him throughout all eternity as brothers and sisters, joint heirs with Him in God's adopted family. I don't think the good news can get any better than that.

Questions for Reflection

1. *Of whom does Isaiah 53 speak?*

2. *Can you explain the simplicity of the gospel?*

3. *What's so good about the good news?*

4. *What was our relationship with God before we received Christ? How about after?*

5. *Should I even have told those ladies I had gotten a speeding ticket?*

Suggested Resources

The Gospel According to Jesus by John MacArthur Jr. Zondervan Publishing House, 1994.

Knowing God by J.I. Packer. InterVarsity Press, 1993.

Through the Windows of Heaven by Walter Martin and Jill Martin Rische. Broadman & Holman Publishers, 1999.

Seizing the
Opportunities:
How My Life Is My Witness

🐂

y nose hurt. No kidding…my nose actually hurt from
smelling all those candles. I simply couldn't make up my mind—the
selection was outrageous. Perhaps you can identify if you've ever been
to one of those candle parties and sniffed your way to a sore nose. Even
coffee grounds didn't clear away the sassy-but-nice pumpkin-spice
scent from my nasal passages.

The following week I received an invitation to a home-and-garden
party—two weeks later, a cookware party. A week after I had spent 20
bucks for a spatula, I was invited to a cosmetics party. I had never
imagined that the ladies in this little community could be such party
animals, but there I was, invited to one in-home shopping party after
another, after another. It was remarkable how each hostess was just as
excited as the next regarding her offering of wares. That excitement
was catching. At the candle party, after the speaker revealed the plan
for how we could become sales representatives as well, a few women
took advantage of the offer. Several other women signed up to host a
party in their homes, and out went the circle of invitations all over
again. So if my nose wasn't sore enough the first time around, surely
I'd have two or three more opportunities.

I must say, I did have a lot of fun. However, the majority of women
at those parties were believers—and I couldn't help but think,
Wouldn't it be great to offer the best plan of all right here and now? What
amazed me was how eager each hostess was to tell us gals about her

party and the different items we might have the opportunity to purchase. Suddenly these women, and many others just like them, became bold spokeswomen—apologists, if you will, for their in-home shopping parties.

Oddly enough, the great majority of women I talk with about sharing the Lord usually comment, "Oh, I'm not comfortable talking to people about the Lord. I'm just not gifted in that area." Then they quickly end our conversation with "My life is my witness" or "I'm a silent witness." How unfortunate it is that many women who can speak enthusiastically about an in-home shopping party feel they can't adequately communicate their testimony for Christ.

I hear this quite a bit when attempting to encourage women to share the gospel. I know the Holy Spirit will give them the tools they need—and surely there is nothing more exciting to share than the hope of redemption. But it sometimes seems to me that the comment "My life is my witness" or "I'm a silent witness" is offered more as an excuse to remain silent than as a tactic for winning souls for eternity.

By definition, a witness, however, cannot be silent. A witness is someone who attests to a fact or event. A witness is one who gives public testimony, one who furnishes proof. That is the definition of the word *witness*. Yes, our life is a witness—it's the loudest witness we have. If Christianity is true it should permeate every area of our life. Nevertheless, as witnesses, we must also give public testimony—we must furnish proof for what we have witnessed.

Being a witness is not as hard as you might think. The purpose of this chapter is to encourage you to let your life, which includes your verbal proclamation, be a powerful witness in three distinct areas: the home, the church, and the world.

How My Life Is My Witness in the Home

My husband and I have a little arrangement. He takes care of the outside of the home while I take care of the inside. He mows, I vacuum. He deals with the overgrown ferns and thistle—I take care of the over-grown stack of dishes in the sink and laundry in the hamper. He plants and waters, I decorate. Now, I happen to think I got the better end of the deal, because I love decorating. Since I am a bargain-hunter through and through, I feel I've achieved quite a victory whenever I find something cute that fits in just the right spot...for under 20 bucks. It's a conquest. Usually when I make a significant find, I am immediately on the telephone to my mother-in-law, scoring points for being a wise wife with the cold hard cash her son worked so hard to earn.

Now, as the decorator of the home, I understand how important it is to attend those candle parties. My children love the fragrance of spice during the holidays—and in the spring, a nice floral scent. The fragrance in the home is a pretty important thing. Yet what is more important to the house I desire to make into a home is the aroma of my life. Second Corinthians 2:14 reads, "Thanks be to God, who always leads us in His triumph in Christ, and manifests through us the sweet aroma of the knowledge of Him in every place."

"The knowledge of Him in every place." I think one of the best ways to manifest His knowledge in our favorite place is to fulfill the call of Deuteronomy 6:4-7:

> *Hear, O Israel! The LORD is our God, the LORD is one! You shall love the LORD your God with all your heart and with all your soul and with all your might. These words, which I am commanding you today, shall be on your heart. You shall teach them diligently to your sons and shall talk of them when you sit in your house and when you walk by the way and when you lie down and when you rise up.*

What a great and high calling it is to pass our faith on to our children, to be a life witness in the home to those hearts tender toward God and those spirits sensitive to Him. How wonderful it is that, though God has given us such a sober charge in Deuteronomy 6, He has readied the soil for the seed of our witness.

I am constantly amazed at how spiritual small children can be. When Nicole was quite tiny, I used to quote to her—and in a very dramatic fashion—John 1:1-5,14. Remembering that I had done this with Nicole, one day I decided to recite it just as dramatically to our three-year-old son, Mikael.

> *In the beginning was the Word, and the Word was with God, and the Word was God. He was in the beginning with God. All things came into being through Him, and apart from Him nothing came into being that has come into being. In Him was life,*

> *and the life was the Light of men. The Light shines in the dark-*
> *ness, and the darkness did not comprehend it.*
>   *...And the Word became flesh, and dwelt among us, and we*
> *saw His glory, glory as of the only begotten from the Father, full*
> *of grace and truth.*

He was mesmerized. When I finished, simply for curiosity's sake—because I had never explained it to him—I asked, "Mikael, who is the Word?" He said, without a moment's hesitation and with as much passion as he could muster, "Jesus! And He is alive, and He *wose fron da* dead, and He is alive!" I was stunned.

We are to diligently teach our children the things of the Lord. It is impossible to do that silently, especially since we are commanded to "talk of them when you sit in your house and when you walk by the way and when you lie down and when you rise up." We are to seize every moment we can as an opportunity to plant the Word of God and to cultivate a genuine love for Him in their hearts.

You might be thinking, *But Judy, aren't most things caught, not taught to our children?* This is quite true. That is why we must not forget the first part of Deuteronomy 6: "You shall love the LORD your God with all your heart and with all your soul and with all your might." The children are indeed watching. And if you don't have small children, perhaps you have grandchildren—or perhaps you have an aged parent or an unbelieving husband in the home. Whichever the case may be, someone is watching you.

Truly, our love for and devotion to God are even more contagious than the excitement of a candle party. Moreover, an excitement for God prompts our verbal witness. We just can't help it. Oh, how important it is for that true-love devotion to be in our hearts so we can be the witness in our home, day to day, that the Lord calls us to be.

The Woman in the Mirror

One of the things I love about a life in Christ is that it is not a shallow existence. This is especially seen in passages of Scripture like 2 Corinthians 13:5 and Romans 12:2:

> *Test yourselves to see if you are in the faith; examine your-*
> *selves! Or do you not recognize this about yourselves, that Jesus*
> *Christ is in you—unless indeed you fail the test?*

Do not be conformed to this world, but be transformed by the renewing of your mind, so that you may prove what the will of God is, that which is good and acceptable and perfect.

A. W. Tozer posed a wonderful question: "What comes into your mind when you think about God?" He then noted that "worship is pure or base as the worshiper entertains high or low thoughts of God."[1] Before we can hope to be any kind of witness for Christ at all, we must first examine our hearts and be willing to ask ourselves the tough Tozer question.

The Christian life is one of self-examination and reflection. It is a faith that penetrates deep into the inner man or woman, allowing the Lord to do His healing and cleansing work. While this can be a painful process, how wonderful it is to allow the Lord to bring those things before our eyes that we have either justified or denied, so He can help us deal with them. When we are willing even though it might be painful, He moves us toward wholeness and holiness.

This is when those around us witness the radical transformation of a life, and it is the testimony we can't help but verbally proclaim— the glory of God cleansing us from the inside out. (I imagine this is one of the reasons why, when we take the communion cup, we don't pour it over our head. The cup that symbolizes the blood of Christ shed for the cleansing of our sins is taken internally, right where we need it the most.)

Are You Ready to Be Transformed?

Jesus Christ transforms us when we submit to His Lordship— when we see sin as He sees it, and our desire is to do something about it. I was once asked by a seeker, "How can I know what is a sin?" My response was, "Ask the Lord, 'Does this please You?' and wait for His reply." When we wait for the reply and obey His voice, our lives will, thankfully, never be the same.

Ezekiel 11:19-20 is a passage that means a great deal to me:

I will give them one heart, and put a new spirit within them. And I will take the heart of stone out of their flesh and give them a heart of flesh, that they may walk in My statutes and keep My ordinances and do them. Then they will be My people, and I shall be their God.

Though this passage in Ezekiel concerns first the nation of Israel, I am also a living example of God taking a heart of stone and replacing it with a heart of flesh. Before giving my life to Christ, I was quite emotionally detached. I could turn my feelings off like a light switch and literally feel nothing toward another human being outside of myself—except, of course, if they brought some sort of advantage to me. What a horrible, sick existence. I imagine that I must have been at the height of emotional dysfunction.

Though it wasn't an easy process and at times was downright painful, God so transformed my heart that now I find it hard to worship without tears streaming down my face. She who hadn't cried for years now finds it hard to get through a 20-minute song service. Somehow, when I feel those tears upon my cheeks I am reminded of the miracle God performed in my life. How can I remain silent?

So how are you doing in the self-examination department? Do you profess Jesus Christ as Lord, yet your life seems to go on like business as usual? While I was on the road as a sales representative, in a small hotel room in Morgan Hill, California, all by my lonesome, I decided to pick up that Gideon Bible. That night I read 1 John 2:4, and I was immediately convicted. When I wrestled with the truth of that passage, it drove me to serious self-examination, and then to my knees. "The one who says, 'I have come to know Him,' and does not keep His commandments, is a liar, and the truth is not in him."

Ouch! No Lordship, no life change...and ultimately the trinity I worshiped was *me, myself, and I*. However, once the Lord truly took residence in my heart, the results were a radical transformation and a passionate love for God.

When we allow the Lord to cleanse and heal us, day by day we pursue His presence like never before. "If anyone is in Christ, he is a new creature; the old things passed away; behold, new things have come."[2] As new creatures in Christ, we find that He suddenly becomes the delight of our everyday conversation. We cannot help but speak of Him to others.

How many brides have you known who did not constantly speak of their betrothed? Have you ever met a bride who was not longing for her wedding day? Since, as believers, we are referred to in the Scriptures as the bride of Christ, how about you? Are you a bride who loves to talk about your Groom, one who longs for her wedding day? I pray this is the case.

As Christians, we are called to a life of self-examination and refining. We come to Him with one thing only, a broken and contrite heart—which He, thankfully, replaces and then fills with a burning desire to love and serve Him with all our heart, soul, mind, and strength. Those who live with us day by day cannot ignore the transformation in our lives because of that refining process. May our passion and love for God be a contagious flame that ignites a fire in their hearts as well.

How My Life Is My Witness in the Church

I love my sisters in the Lord. We are a family indeed. This too is evidence of the radical transformation that God performed in my life. God has given me such a heart and love not only for my sisters in Christ, but for my sisters in Adam as well: one group to encourage in the Lord, the other to lead to His love, forgiveness, freedom, and gift of eternal life.

My sisters in Christ have taught me so much—I am indebted to them. What would I have done had they not shared their gift of hospitality so that an old corporate woman could learn how to be a loving hostess? What would I do without my sisters who love our kids and willingly baby-sit when my husband and I need a night out together, or when the Lord calls me to minister in another city?

The love we share is genuine, unwavering, and supernatural. When I speak to a group I am almost heartbroken to leave, I love my sisters so. It does not matter that I have just met them that weekend—I love them all. I love listening to them share their hearts, and I am humbled when God grants me an opportunity to offer a word of encouragement or pray for them about a particular need, from weight loss to a wayward child. What a blessing it is to receive a note in the mail from a woman I have prayed with, telling me what God has accomplished in some particular matter. This sort of thing is our life witness in the church, and it is the fulfillment of 1 John 4:7:

> *Beloved, let us love one another, for love is from God; and everyone who loves is born of God and knows God. The one who does not love does not know God, for God is love. By this the love*

> *of God was manifested in us, that God has sent His only begotten Son into the world so that we might live through Him. In this is love, not that we loved God, but that He loved us and sent His Son to be the propitiation for our sins. Beloved, if God so loved us, we also ought to love one another.*

Indeed, we ought to love one another. Yet, like any family, we sure can have our little scraps and disagreements. Nevertheless, the Holy Spirit is the tie that binds our hearts in one accord, and our response to one another is unique to the church of Jesus Christ. I will never forget, on my 1994 trip to Russia, holding the face of a young Russian woman as tears streamed down our faces for joy of the love of God. Though we could not communicate with words, our hearts and spirits spoke volumes. This is a love I wish the whole world knew, a love many would never think possible—and it isn't, apart from an abiding relationship with God.

The Witness of Unity

Colossians 3:12-17 encourages us to remember who we are in the family of God and how we ought to respond to one another:

> *As those who have been chosen of God, holy and beloved, put on a heart of compassion, kindness, humility, gentleness and patience; bearing with one another, and forgiving each other, whoever has a complaint against anyone; just as the Lord forgave you, so also should you. Beyond all these things put on love, which is the perfect bond of unity. Let the peace of Christ rule in your hearts, to which indeed you were called in one body; and be thankful. Let the word of Christ richly dwell within you, with all wisdom teaching and admonishing one another with psalms and hymns and spiritual songs, singing with thankfulness in your hearts to God. Whatever you do in word or deed, do all in the name of the Lord Jesus, giving thanks through Him to God the Father.*

If I had only one single short opportunity to encourage women to let their lives be a powerful witness in the church, I think I would simply quote Philippians 2:1-2 since the Scriptures always say it best:

If there is any encouragement in Christ, if there is any consolation of love, if there is any fellowship of the Spirit, if any affection and compassion, make my joy complete by being of the same mind, maintaining the same love, united in spirit, intent on one purpose.

And may that purpose be to glorify God in all we say and do before everyone, whether they are in Christ or in Adam. This is our life witness in the church—it is obvious to all that our love is genuine, tangible, unwavering, and without hypocrisy—a love that is indeed a supernatural gift of God.

How My Life Is My Witness in the World

One of the advantages of having left the corporate world to become a mom who's full-time in the home is that I have an opportunity to Christmas-shop during the week, when everyone else is at the office. Unfortunately, as you know, the closer it gets to midnight on Christmas Eve, the busier the shopping malls become. One such holiday season, which I will never forget, Nicole and I decided to venture out to a large mall for a few last-minute gifts...two days before Christmas. What a madhouse! It seemed to me that no matter what stores we tried, we happened upon crowds that were thick and lines that were long. After a while, my stomach told me it was time for lunch, so we decided to grab a bite to eat.

The timing was perfect. As one couple left a sandwich-shop counter, we managed to settle into their now-empty seats. A cheery young lady waited on us, and it struck me how graciously she handled the crowds while maintaining a bright smile. Apparently my daughter noticed it as well. Nicole leaned into me and whispered, "She's really nice, isn't she?"

"Yes, Honey, she sure is," I agreed as I sank my teeth into my sandwich. After a few minutes, I noticed my daughter trying to get her attention. As the young lady raced back and forth, happily filling her customer's orders, Nicole kept patiently saying, "E'scuse me...e'scuse me." Finally, the lady heard my five-year-old's soft voice and asked, "Oh, I'm sorry—did you need something?"

"Can I ask you a question?" Nicole asked eagerly.

"Sure," came her expectant reply.

"Do...do you know Jesus?"

Somewhat startled, then looking at me, she said, "Well, yeah...I guess so...I mean...I've been to catechism and all." Then leaning close to Nicole's face she said, "Yeah, I guess I do."

Nicole's countenance radiated joy, and looking as if she were about to burst, she energetically stated, "I *love* Him!" The young lady's face turned beet-red. She could plainly see that this little girl loved God, and not only that, but that she couldn't wait to tell others. Suddenly it became very difficult for me to swallow my turkey-and-cheese-on-wheat with that large lump in the middle of my throat.

When our life is our witness in the home, it certainly influences the world around us—just as much as if we were out there ourselves. Nicole's beaming love for Jesus and her desire to be His witness to others in the world around her makes me so want to follow the charge that Jesus gives to all believers in Matthew 28:18-20:

> *All authority has been given to Me in heaven and on earth. Go therefore and make disciples of all the nations, baptizing them in the name of the Father and the Son and the Holy Spirit, teaching them to observe all that I commanded you; and lo, I am with you always, even to the end of the age.*

Jesus has called us to bear fruit for the kingdom. He has called us to the awesome task of making disciples, or students, of the Lord and His Word—not merely moving folks to an intellectual assent but to a vibrant relationship with Him. We are to help those we lead to Christ to grow in their faith and knowledge of Him so they can then make disciples of others whom they lead to Christ.

Perhaps you are married but don't have children, or perhaps you have grown children and are an empty-nester. Perhaps you are a single woman—a corporate woman as I once was. Oh, how mightily God can use you at your place of business. I can't help but think of one friend of mine who, after realizing she was surrounded by other believers at her place of work, decided to start a once-a-week prayer meeting before the day began.

What a wonderful impact it is making, especially since she works at a county prison. Knowing that she and other believers meet for prayer, other co-workers—whom she never anticipated would talk with her about her faith—have unexpectedly approached her. My friend is more than happy to meet with them after work and is available to do so now that her kids are off to college. Though she's a bit intimidated at times, she is thrilled with the opportunities she's having...and she never imagined God would use her in this way.

We're Equipped for an Exciting Assignment

Answering the call of the great cmmission can seem overwhelming, but our Lord and Savior never calls us to a task without adequately equipping us to accomplish it. How blessed we are to live in a nation where we have access to a wealth of resources to help us become better equipped or more confident in fulfilling Jesus' command. In fact, I cannot help but feel that we will be held a bit more accountable because of the overwhelming amount of access we have to Christian radio, Christian bookstores, and faithful fellowships.

The apostle Peter wrote, "Sanctify Christ as Lord in your hearts, always being ready to make a defense to everyone who asks you to give an account for the hope that is in you, yet with gentleness and reverence."[3] That charge is complemented by what the apostle Paul wrote in Colossians 4:5-6: "Conduct yourselves with wisdom toward outsiders, making the most of the opportunity. Let your speech always be with grace, as though seasoned with salt, so that you will know how you should respond to each person." When I think of what these two passages must look like as part of our life witness, I am reminded of my children's favorite storybook, *The Pilgrim's Progress* by John Bunyan. Bunyan's book is a wonderful example of the believer's walk in this world. It's filled with challenges to the faith and sound answers to those challenges. The life of Christian (the pilgrim) is one of testifying for the Lord, a life of defending his faith uncompromisingly yet graciously.

Being a life witness in this world is not always a comfortable or easy thing to do. Fortunately, Jesus knew that going into all the world would be a challenging prospect—one that would require nothing less than being filled with the Holy Spirit and His power. Where is this more needed than when we testify of the Lord to our closest family and friends—those who remember us before we became new in Christ? Jesus said, "A prophet is not without honor except in his own hometown, and in his own household."[4]

Yes, it isn't easy sharing the Lord, but it sure is exciting. Some missionaries we support in Sudan, whose lives are always in danger, tell us with great confidence that they are "living the book of Acts." I am reminded of Philippians 3:14: "I press on toward the goal for the prize of the upward call of God in Christ Jesus."

Indeed, we press on. Does the Lord call all of us to travel to distant lands? No. Does He call each one of us to write a book or speak before thousands of people? No. Would He like us to seize the divine appointments He places before us in our home or neighborhood, our workplace or grocery store, on the job, or perhaps right at our own front door? You bet.

God is on the move, and He wants us to join Him in reaching the lost for eternity, rescuing individuals from a state of sin and death to bring them into a glorious life in Christ. What a wonderful opportunity we have to join the fray! True faith in God is not passive, it's active, as Stephen Charnock notes: "God is active, because He is spirit; and if we be like to God, the more spiritual we are, the more active we shall be."[5]

The great commission is just that. It is great. Though it can seem overwhelming, nonetheless, by God's grace our hearts can be set on fire for those who don't know Him. We each have been granted a job to do as siblings in the family of God, because

> how...will they call on Him in whom they have not believed? How will they believe in Him whom they have not heard? And how will they hear without a preacher? How will they preach unless they are sent? Just as it is written, "How beautiful are the feet of those who bring good news of good things!"[6]

May the Lord give you grace as you bring your beautiful feet to those who need Him—those who are right under your nose.

Final Thoughts

Philosophy professor J.P. Moreland, a brilliant author, thinker, and Christian apologist, wrote the following in regard to what it meant for him to be a follower of Jesus Christ:

> I repeatedly return to the conviction that Jesus of Nazareth is simply peerless. He is the wisest, most virtuous, most influential

person in history. I can't even imagine what the last two thousand years would have been like without His influence. There is no one remotely like Him. The power of His ideas, the quality of His character, the beauty of His personality, the uniqueness of His life, miracles, crucifixion, and resurrection are so far removed from any other person or ideology that, in my view, it is the greatest honor ever bestowed on me to be counted among His followers.

Not only is it an unspeakable honor to be one of His followers, it is also by far the greatest opportunity to gain a life of meaning and to become what we all know we ought to be.[7]

I cannot say it better than Dr. Moreland. Jesus Christ brought us to a place of reconciliation with God. In Him, we've been freed from the bondage of a life of sin, the bondage of the terror of death, and the bondage of an intuitive knowledge of God's wrath through judgment.

> *God, being rich in mercy, because of His great love with which He loved us, even when we were dead in our transgressions, made us alive together with Christ (by grace you have been saved), and raised us up with Him, and seated us with Him in the heavenly places in Christ Jesus, so that in the ages to come He might show the surpassing riches of His grace in kindness toward us in Christ Jesus.*[8]

How can we remain silent in the face of that?

When you share the blessed truth of the gospel of Jesus Christ, questions usually arise. I pray that this guide will help you answer them. I also pray that you will take time to read the resources I've suggested. How glorious it is to be used by God—and it *is* His desire to use you.

I find that reasons for my faith and the opportunity to share them produce confidence in God, which displaces fear that leads to bondage. In fact, I sincerely think that if more believing women would grasp the importance of knowing what they believe and why, many self-help books would be rendered unnecessary.

Perhaps you have friends or family members who believe, yet still struggle in their lives and in their faith. It's true—life sure can seem to toss us to and fro. Yet I find that when circumstances of my life become more difficult and the thistle does hit my chin, then having sound reasons for my faith is something tangible in the midst of uncertainty. Sound reasons for faith are a wonderful reminder that the God I serve and the faith I hold are as rock-solid as the Chief Cornerstone in whom I have never been disappointed. Nor will I ever be.

> For I am convinced that neither death, nor life, nor angels, nor principalities, nor things present, nor things to come, nor powers, nor height, nor depth, nor any other created thing, will be able to separate us from the love of God, which is in Christ Jesus our Lord.[9]

Questions for Reflection

1. What is the command of Deuteronomy 6:4-9?

2. What does a life in Christ call you to in regard to the inner woman?

3. How can your life be a witness in your church?

4. What is the great commission?

5. When was the last time your beautiful feet brought the good news to someone else?

Suggested Resources

Love Your God with All Your Mind: The Role of Reason in the Life of the Soul by J.P. Moreland. NavPress Publishing Group, 1997.

A Time to Speak by Judy Salisbury. Logos Presentations, 2001.

Pictorial Pilgrim's Progress by John Bunyan, illus. Joanne Brubaker. Moody Press, 1960.

About the Author

Judy Salisbury speaks nationally on a wide variety of subjects from Christian apologetics to Christian living, and is a popular speaker for conferences, women's retreats, youth rallies, and general assemblies. As the founder of Logos Presentations, she specializes in training Christian leaders to communicate their message more effectively and also in training them to teach other believers how to reach those who may be hostile or ambivalent toward the gospel of Jesus Christ.

Judy has also created the unique, informative, and entertaining compact-disc series *Divine Appointments: Spontaneous Conversations on Matters of the Heart, Soul, and Mind,* designed as an easy method to help equip Christian women with answers to common questions regarding their faith. In addition to this, she has authored a communication training manual, *A Time to Speak;* she is also a contributing author of *Is Your Church Ready?: Motivating Leaders to Live an Apologetic Life* (co-edited by Ravi Zacharias and Dr. Norman Geisler).

For more information, write to:
Logos Presentations
11500 NE 76th Street, Building A-3, Suite 202
Vancouver, WA 98662
Or send an e-mail to:
logos@wa-net.com